For Nathan, Isaac, and Hannah, with my stellar love: entrepreneurship mindset is a lavish road to freedom.

For my Dad who would have loved to read this.

2019, November 11

Greetings

Special thanks to those who encouraged me to achieve this book, and contributed greatly to its improvements by their careful reading, and innovation expertise: Jean-François Caillard, Lena Engelmann, Véronique Bouchard, Dominique van Deth, Raphaël Thobie, Fabien Canitrot, Olivier Schwartz.

Deep gratitude to the top-notch intrapreneurs who accepted to share their experiences, and to their intrapreneurship managers who connected me to them: their testimonial is beyond price.

This book wouldn't have his flesh without the openness, conviction, and experience sharing of the corporate innovation and intrapreneurship managers from over 40 companies. May they be thanked for their active role in intrapreneurship soaring.

D1525422

Preface 1

Startups fail because they struggle to find customers. Corporates fail because they stop talking to their own customers. Learning from customers is ever so important in today's world where we are more connected to customers than ever before.

Companies that outlearn their competition win. Period. So why is this difficult?

In theory, corporates should never lose against startups because they have more resources and access to customers. The reason they do is they often can't match the agility of a startup. Speed of learning is the new unfair advantage and going fast requires a new playbook.

Nicolas' book delivers just that. It's full of concrete examples, recipes, and tactics from some of the top corporates in the world. It will inspire you to start or refine your intrapreneurship journey in the right direction.

Ash Maurya - Author of Running Lean and Scaling Lean, creator of Lean Canvas, Product Builder for over a decade, and founder of LEANSTACK

Preface 2

Nicolas Bry is a seasoned practitioner, and a top French expert in intrapreneurship. He is also a talented blogger (rapidinnovation.fr), speaker, and networker.

His recent opus perfectly reflects the depth and breadth of his experience. In his "Intrapreneurs' Factory" handbook, Nicolas develops a 10-step approach that addresses the major issues and challenges that arise when implementing intrapreneurship. For each step, he lists the key questions, and proposes a wealth of recent examples that constitute a great source of inspiration.

In the last part of his handbook, Nicolas summarizes the story of over 20 intrapreneurs who have very different goals, profiles, and stories but share a passion: turning an idea into something of lasting value for their company, and beyond.

I read "The Intrapreneurs' Factory" from beginning to end, and I know I will often open it again when confronting a specific issue or in search of an inspiring example.

Véronique Bouchard, Ph.D. - Full Professor at emlyon business school, and Intrapreneurship Expert

Table of content

Introduction

The Intrapreneurs' Factory is a practical guide for corporate managers who want to leverage intrapreneurship for their business, employees, and the greater good.

It targets **managers in innovation, intrapreneurship, open innovation, new business and development, or strategic managers**. Considering the human dimension of intrapreneurship, it also addresses **managers in organizational / cultural transformation, HR, and digital** (digital culture and tools being a cornerstone in the company transformation).

This guide provides them with **10 pragmatic steps to design an intrapreneurship approach**, based on the return of experience of 40 recent intrapreneurship programs. These 10 lighthouses aim at guiding corporate managers in shaping their **own path** of intrapreneurship, the specific path that will fit with their company.

3 steps are particularly delicate to negotiate: sponsorship, intrapreneurs' coaching, and business units commitment. Moreover, these are persisting steps: intrapreneurship manager must keep in the loop the corresponding stakeholders: sponsors, intrapreneurs, and business units.

To capture the big picture of intrapreneurship, 3 factors have to be considered beyond the program 'stricto sensu':

- Combining intrapreneurship with pre-existing devices of the **corporate innovation ecosystem**;
- Blending project delivery with the **key human aspects** at stake, from selecting the right intrapreneurs profile, coaching them, to supporting the development of their skills and career;
- Incorporating the **societal impact wave**: intrapreneurship is a true surfboard for balancing profitability with sustainability.

To illustrate intrapreneurship value creation, you will discover over **20 meaningful stories of intrapreneurs**: they utterly illustrate business and human output of the factory.

This playbook is pragmatic, it balances **intrapreneurship advocacy with the approach of an objective innovation expert**. It is simply drafted, as if we had a conversation with our readers.

WHAT IT IS NOT

It is not an academic research book on intrapreneurship: for this, we are keen readers of the Corporate Entrepreneurship book, written by Véronique Bouchard with the contribution of Alain Fayolle. Véronique's work explores comprehensively the various facets of corporate entrepreneurship, and highlights intrapreneurship enablers.

It is not a scientific thesis where, according to defined inputs, it would design the perfect program for intrapreneurs fitting your company. I advocate for free-will, and timely maturation of the intrapreneurship manager, to work out the program. Giving an attentive look at the risks underlined at each step, you will nevertheless capture the 'must have', and evacuate the ancillary features.

It is not focused on transitioning the intrapreneurs' projects into business, namely scaling corporate startups. The Scaling-up Corporate Startups book, written by Frank Mattes and Dr. Ralph-Christian Ohr, addresses the topic. In a way, The Intrapreneur Fabric is a prequel to Scaling-up Corporate Startups!

SCOPE

The term intrapreneurship was coined in the 80s with the definition by Pinchot in 1984 : Intrapreneurship = **intra-company entrepreneurship**.

Entrepreneurship is the capacity and willingness to develop, organize, and manage a business venture along with any of its risks in order to make a profit.

When translating intrapreneurship in the act of behaving like an entrepreneur while working within a large organization, Steve Jobs remembered the startups he worked with as a young man... "**a group of people going back to the garage, but in a large company**."

Some companies have supported exemplary intrapreneur initiatives:

- 3M with the "15% time" program (**3M Bootleg** rule): R&D employees are allowed to spend 15% of their time on personal projects). It lead to the business success of post-its and its developer Arthur Fry, building on a former invention by Spencer Silver;
- **Google 20%** time allocation: all IT developers can spend 20% of their time, or one day a week, working on a project of their choice; it gave birth to astonishing services: Gmail (Paul Buchheit's innovation), Google Maps, Google News, and it is said even AdSense, Google cash cow in advertising! Twitter, Slack, and Groupon also started as side projects. Google believes that people are **more productive** when they are working on things that they consider important or that they have invented; Google has set-up in 2016 a Startup Lab, Area 120, to incubate intrapreneurs' project; it works in

coordination with Google Ventures so as to fund smoothly projects that would spin-out;

- **Facebook Like button** is the output of an internal hackathon, and the brilliant idea of a multidisciplinary team of 5 Facebook employees, which managed to overpass a first disastrous review with CEO Mark Zuckerberg;
- Sony with Ken Kutaragi, the intrapreneur unearthing the **PlayStation** business;
- ETA Manufacture Horlogère with Elmar Mock, the **Swatch**'s (Swiss Made Watch) inventor.

Further definitions have emerged:

- **Corporate Entrepreneurship** is the development of new business ideas and opportunities within large and established corporations (Birkinshaw, 2003);
- Corporate Entrepreneurship refers to an **undertaking team** developing new businesses within established firms, somehow different from the core business (Bouchard, 2018). This last definition shows the overarching role played by the intrapreneurs' team in the process.

Intrapreneurship is not hype: it has been running for nearly 40 years now. But intrapreneurship has blossomed more recently with a stress on structured corporate programs, aiming at organizing, and facilitating the intrapreneur path.

This book spots most **recent initiatives**, to capture the best practices in setting-up top-notch intrapreneurship devices.

Do intrapreneurs exist without programs for intrapreneurs? Surely, and they can achieve feats! But we are strong believers they thrive when the corporation makes it a little bit easier, and shapes a supportive framework, taking advantage of the present guide.

Ten steps to shape a resounding program for intrapreneurs

In the next chapters, we dig into ten steps to customize your intrapreneurship approach to unfold **new business lines**, and support intrapreneurs' prowess, tutoring them and transforming them into **agents of change**.

Each step is structured as follows:

- The Challenge you have to solve in this step;
- Uses Cases: corporate examples to inspire you, how other companies do it;
- Key Questions: peruse this list, and provide an answer to the questions to solve the challenge;
- The Main Risk to carefully vet in this step.

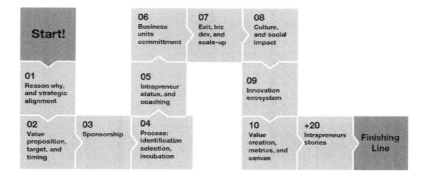

The workflow is ordered logically, but it is nothing but a mandatory route, and you can jump directly to the steps which are of the most interest to you.

Nevertheless, it's by **composing with these 10 levers together** that you will put intrapreneurship on the best tracks in your company.

Step 1: Reason why, and strategic alignment

CHALLENGE

Here, the challenge that you have to overpass is to describe which **problem intrapreneurship is solving**, in other words explain the 'reason why', and then the purpose of the program. From there, you will look for **strategic alignment with the corporation** so that intrapreneurship is embedded in the corporation in a sustainable way.

USE CASES

>> WHY?

How Deutsche Telekom, Bouygues, Deutsche Bahn, Orange, Air France do it

One can imagine **a variety of purposes** for setting-up an intrapreneurship approach:

⬎ Deutsche Telekom Incubator VP, Johannes Nuenning, explains that UQbate is targeting employees who want to realize their idea, and **become entrepreneurs**: yes, en-trepreneur, and not necessarily in-trapreneur!

↘ Bouygues "Innovate like a startup" is an intrapreneurship program to help the Group **reinvent its business** activities shares Vincent Maret, Corporate Director Open Innovation: drawing on the creativity of employees to invent, and roll out solutions meeting the great challenges of the 21st century.

↘ Deutsche Bahn intrapreneurship is **for employees, and business units**. Tobias Taut, Venture Architect, describes its 2 clear goals:

- Creating **new digital business models** which generate new revenues with DB-external companies, hence diversifying DB's product portfolio;
- **Enabling employees** in user-centered and agile methodologies as well as entrepreneurship, fostering long-term cultural change.

↘ Orange problem was to solve the transformation of creative ideas into tangible new business. Therefore its program for intrapreneurs stresses on **ideas implementation**.

↘ Air France VP Innovation & Intrapreneurship Programs, Marine Gall, explains her program is at the **crossroads of transformation, and business**. The objective is to develop new business with an innovative approach, to offer an ecosystem to teams that have an initiative, want to commit, and take responsibility.

↘ For a French media company who's currently setting up intrapreneurship, its purpose is to give a boost to its employees' **motivation**, while for an insurance company, its reason why is to be **more reactive** on bringing new products to the market.

KEY QUESTIONS

To define the 'reason why', and set intrapreneurship purpose in stone in your company business, review this series of questions.

>> PURPOSE

Does your reason why / purpose borrows to:

- Bringing new products and services to market more quickly, with less risk of failure, and improving customer/prospects intimacy, understanding closely their problems?
- Protecting your business against startups aiming to disrupt your business model?
- Retaining your best staff, and groom the leaders, equipped with a nimble way to innovate?
- Creating an environment where new ideas can be systematically tested and iterated until they fit the market, and the company culture?
- Making a societal impact, and linking with CSR policy?

>> CORPORATE HISTORY, AND BUSINESS ALIGNMENT

- Has the company a track-record in intrapreneurship as well as in entrepreneurship?
- Are some managers renowned entrepreneurs?
- How will the business priorities / issues be incorporated in the program for intrapreneurs (aka during the request for ideas, in the selection criteria, and jury - Selection stage in step 4)?
- How is intrapreneurship matching the corporate strategy? Is intrapreneurship part of the annual company report? Of the corporate values charter?
- Is the top management committed to speak about the program?
- Are the corporate communication channels ready to relay intrapreneurship information?

>> BUDGET, AND IMPACT

- Is a budget dedicated to intrapreneurship?
- Does it cover program for intrapreneurs facilitation (coordinating team), and resources to perform the projects?
- How is measured the impact of intrapreneurship?
- What are the measurable objectives of the program? (in the Metrics stage in step 10, we will see how it is important to define the objectives before launching the program for intrapreneurs)

MAIN RISK

One frequent risk consists in **eluding the problem at stake**, and lay out a lackluster program without clear objectives and identity: if the purpose is not focused, it will not be folded in the company DNA.

Step 2: Value proposition for intrapreneurs, target group, and timing

CHALLENGE

 The challenge consists in expressing **the value proposition** of the program for its **target employees**, the benefits it will bring to employees, as well as the pain relievers. Similarly, you will review the benefits for the partnering business units. Last but not least you will draft the **overarching roadmap** or key milestones for the intrapreneurs.

USES CASES

>> VALUE PROPOSITION

How Orange, Oracle, Air France do it

Most programs for intrapreneurs are open to all employees as they embrace a movement of crowd-innovation. But according to their purpose, some can zoom on specific employees.

↘ Orange France Petite Fabrique (Small Factory) targets recently hired employees, below 30, because the purpose implies **on-boarding of new employees**. The program interconnects them, and opens them the doors to innovation, through inspiration, introspection (team skills, and problem to solve), and action phases, up to a pitch in front of the executive committee.

The value proposition for the employees frequently consists in the possibility to **implement its idea into the daily business of the group**. It combines **autonomy** (free time for the employee to work on his idea), **resources** (staffing of an innovation team, and budget), **coaching** (guiding the intrapreneur, and helping him overcome the obstacles), **localization** in an innovation space.

⬐ Orange Group intrapreneurs' studio value proposition is to support any employee, with an innovation idea for Orange business, in implementing it with the help of a BU sponsor. Support addresses the success of the project, but also the personal development of the intrapreneur.

Value proposition to engage employees in entrepreneurship mindset can embrace other miscellaneous forms:

⬐ Oracle, and its previous Corporate Responsibility & Open Innovation manager, Dominique van Deth, involves employees in its open innovation program with startups: **Bring Your Own Startup**, where employees can promote themselves a startup using their own networks, and **Adopt a**

Startup, where they can choose from a selection of already sourced startups;

⌄ Orange Belgium **Innovation Squad program,** led by Innovation Manager, and Head of Orange Fab, Juliette Malherbe, engages employees by connecting them to a selection of startups, and supporting a joint-design of use cases: one startup is accelerated with 4 employees over 6 months, 1/2 day per week;

⌄ Orange Slovakia participates to a cross-companies program named **Butterfly Effect program**; Butterfly Effect facilitates a 5 months incubation (business model canvas, customer research, prototype, design, Ux testing with customers,..) focused on the delivery of a mobile app / mobile game addressing a specific brief/problem, expressed by a participant company.

Regarding the value proposition, another area is the skills certification. Intrapreneurs experience lead to a prowess as innovation leader that can be certified.

⌄ Orange has set-up with **HEC Business School an intrapreneur skills certificate** at the end of intrapreneurs' incubation. Intrapreneurs have to put together in an essay what has been their learning experience on innovation methods, leadership, team management, networking, and ability to make alliances within the corporation. They present it to a mixed jury, composed of Orange and HEC representatives. This certificate is a nifty asset for future jobs demanding leadership, networking and innovation skills.

A few companies have set-up financial incentives for intrapreneurship.

⊾ Air France manages an incentive, congruent to 'Boost the Future' incitation process, which varies from 200 to 1,700 € according to the time spent on the project, and the performance.

>> TIMING, AND THEMATIC

How Telefonica, Lufthansa do it

Classic program milestones are: **identifying intrapreneurs, selecting, and incubating** them with their projects; this process takes place once or twice a year in what is called an Intrapreneurs **Season**.

⊾ Telefonica Head of Innovation Portfolio-Product Innovation, Susana Jurado, runs one or 2 **Innovation Calls** a year. Selected intrapreneurs follow 5 steps: ideation, prototype, beta, products, and scale-up.

Request for intrapreneurs' applications can recall the **strategic axes of development** of the company; they can zoom on **specific thematic**, or can be left wide open to employees' creativity. The right choice depends on the innovation maturity of your employees, Often it helps employees to have a challenge to solve. It depends also on the desire of the business units to commit: they can take part in the theme definition, expressing which issues they would like intrapreneurs to address.

Other companies don't handle seasons, and process intrapreneurship along the way, all year long.

⌐ Lufthansa Systems Business and Innovation Manager, and key executive of the program, Carina Leue-Bensch takes us to the **crowdfunding** path, and a design thinking workshop as for most supported ideas:

- Employees put an idea, and describe pain and gain of the solution. Each employee receives €1000 per year on a virtual account. Once the idea collects €1000 from colleagues (you need 20 employees to support your idea), employees attend a **One day design thinking** workshop. The aim is to design a story with a persona from the user perspective. The output is a 2' video.
- The video will go back to the online tool, and display a budget to receive the financial support. As soon as money is collected (employee can now invest up to 1000 € per idea during an 8 weeks' timeline), the intrapreneur goes to the **Sprint stage**: each intrapreneur follows then a thorough and **bespoke coaching path** to improve his project during a 3

months' timeline: Google Sprint + Business Model Canvas + Pitch Deck + 3 or 4 Demo Days.

The advantage of seasonal calls is to create a momentum, yet you have to attract enough applications, and selection will generate some frustrations. Continuous processing is smoother, but it creates a permanent workload for the intrapreneurship team. One can **spot continuous processing on most popular ideas, and combine it with seasonal events**.

KEY QUESTIONS

This series of questions helps you to define the value proposition, the target group, and the intrapreneurs' roadmap.

>> VALUE PROPOSITION, AND TARGET

- What is the value proposition for the employees, and for the business? Put yourself in the shoes of an employee, and try to answer the question: what's in it for me?
- Will the program provide:
  - o Autonomy (free time)?
  - o Training and coaching (innovation methodology, and mentoring)?
  - o Resources (expertise, and operational contributors to the project)?

25

- Innovation space (a place that enables creative collisions, proximity, diversity and interaction, experimentation, prototyping, and provides facilitation)?
- Protection (a tunnel of goodwill, avoiding a creative idea to be killed right away)?
- Launchpad for career promotion? Ad hoc incentive? Skills recognition?

- Are all employees eligible?
- Have you planned to test the idea of intrapreneurship with employees? With an online questionnaire, or an open event like a barcamp? What are their needs, and pains, and how do you incorporate them in the value proposition?
- What is the value proposition for business units and managers giving away resources:
  - Have you planned to meet some business unit managers to collect their insights (main benefits for business units are listed in the business units' commitment stage, step 6)?
  - Is a manager giving away an intrapreneur allowed to replace him? What are the incentives for him?
  - How manager sharing their resource between daily job, and intrapreneur project will create a fair environment for the intrapreneur?

- Is enticing intrapreneurship part of their manager's role, and will he be positively evaluated if the intrapreneur project is a success?

>> ROADMAP

- What are the successive phases of the program, and key milestones?
- What is the timeline?
- Will you go for seasonal or along the year applications? Will you include business thematics?

MAIN RISK

As in innovation, one substantial risk is to **fall in love with your solution**, and not study enough the user problem; in our case both employees and business units have expectations, and maybe the intrapreneurship approach you have in mind in not exactly the one they are dreaming of.

Step 3: Sponsorship

CHALLENGE

 This challenge is in the top-3 challenges. Here you have to spot the right sponsors: those who will **give a face** to the program, and who will have enough time to **follow-up**, once per quarter, on the intrapreneurs and their projects, and how the program for intrapreneurs pans out.

USES CASES

>> SPONSOR'S ROLE

How Société Générale, Orange do it

↘ Société Générale **CEO,** Frédéric Oudéa, personally stood up to support the intrapreneurship program: the Internal Startup Call. To ensure the engagement of his Executive Committee, he asked **each member to sponsor an intrapreneur project, as if he were a VC** (Venture Capitalist). Wisely he invited those who couldn't find a project, to knock at his door, and explain why they couldn't find a match. Curiously all members find out an intrapreneur project to go with...

⅃ Orange intrapreneurs' studio benefits from **2 sponsors**: the head of the Innovation & Technology division, and the head of Group Transformation, both members of the Executive Committee.

2 sponsors are definitely a security as one sponsor might leave along the way, and leave the program orphaned.

To introduce intrapreneurship to sponsors, one can invite some external program for intrapreneurs' managers to tell their story.

Classic **arguments to embark a sponsor** are related to business impact, employees' engagement, and skills development.

On top of that, one can speak to the heart, recommends Lola Virolle, Intrapreneurship Manager at makesense incubator: going back to the entrepreneurial roots of the company, getting some employees out of the box, and offering them a break in the rush. Propping up the ego, explaining that competitors or innovative new entrants are engaged in intrapreneurship, can hit the nail.

Operational sponsors for the project will be addressed in step 6, business units' commitment.

KEY QUESTIONS

These questions aim at enrolling most relevant sponsor:

- Is the sponsor keen about innovation? Does he have a connection with new business creation, or transformation / human development? Does he add credibility to the program?
- Does he have visibility? Is he part or representative of the Executive Committee?
- Is the sponsor willing to take the floor, and communicate about intrapreneurship?
- Does the sponsor have a good knowledge of the company organization, enabling him to support intrapreneurs in accurate networking?
- Is the sponsor ready to spend some time to support each cohort of intrapreneurs, attending the Jury Selection event or Demo Day at the end of incubation?
- Will he monitor the upshots of the program, and react if it merely has no effect at all? Will he step in in order to alleviate obstacles?

MAIN RISK

One frequent risk is to select a sponsor who is great in terms of visibility but **lacks time to give a hand** to intrapreneurs' projects and program monitoring, or even who is just very difficult to access.

Step 4: Intrapreneurship process: identification, selection, and incubation

CHALLENGE

The challenge here is to define a **detailed framework** that will meet the reason why / purpose, and value proposition that you have set in steps 1 and 2.

We will dig into the roadmap quickly drafted in step 2, Identification/Selection/Incubation. You have defined the What & What For of your program: now it's time to dig into the How.

USE CASES

>> COMMUNICATION, IDENTIFICATION, ON-BOARDING

How Merck, Orange, Swisscom, Tilkee do it

Identification of intrapreneurs starts by building the **awareness** around the intrapreneurship approach, through usual communication channels: presentation on the Intranet, and newsletter, dedicated space on the corporate social network, introduction note by the sponsor, kick-off events... Communication can address directly the employees to trigger applications. They can rely on internal communication channels, and program **ambassadors** who will amplify the message.

⬎ Merck Head of Innovation & Entrepreneurship Incubator, Ulrich Betz, explains how a network of ambassadors in 15 countries was set-up. Innovation friendly, ambassadors relay the innovation spirit, and 3 innovation programs: Innospire which is open to all ideas every 1-2 years and the main funded intrapreneurship device, Open Campaigns which are targeted micro-campaigns every 2-3 months, and Think Tank which has 2 focus areas, and 2 cycles per year. Ambassadors strengthen awareness of the central innovation center, **encourage employee involvement, and spot employees who want to engage**.

Intrapreneurs are not the only target: one shall include specific communication for managers and HR, as well as arguments to attract the business units. In other words, **tailored communication has to be drafted for each target**.

Intrapreneurship is not always familiar to employees.

⬎ Orange facilitates 3 kinds of **pedagogic workshop for employees** who want to know more:

- The first workshop is about the presentation of the program, and the intrapreneurs skills: **reveal your**

intrapreneur potential! Typical **intrapreneurs skills** that participants highlight are: attitude, to be open-minded, brave, acting against the odds, taking a leap of faith despite risks, non-standard thinking, having faith in your ideas, seeing the opportunity, ability to search for allies, being able to cooperate and effective in action;

- The second workshop starts from the intrapreneur idea, and take it to the next stage, using value proposition canvas, and business model canvas, in work group: **come in with an idea, and come out with an innovation project!**

- Finally, Orange facilitates a **Qualification boot camp** with 10 pre-selected projects during 5 days upfront to the jury session. It provides intrapreneurs with the occasion to enrich their concept (value proposition, business model canvas, minimum viable product), let them consider what it means to be an intrapreneur at Orange, and prepare their pitch. It's a smooth way as well to know **the personality of the intrapreneurs** better. Typical way participants describe intrapreneurship is:
  - o Intrapreneurship is the right to innovate for every employee;
  - o It's a tunnel of goodwill;
  - o Intrapreneur is a positive (or diplomatic) rebel, and a jumper of obstacles, he figures

out how to hack the rules... but within the rules' spirit;

    o   He has no super power, but a super desire.

↘ Swisscom Innovation Lab Manager, David Hengartner, has customized a **kick-box**, based on the Adobe kick-box: aspiring intrapreneur can find inside the cardboard box useful canvas to bring his idea to the next level, 20% free time, and a budget credit around 1,000 € that can be spent for the development of the idea.

One can also invite some external intrapreneurship managers, and intrapreneurs to share their story, and interact in an **event** open to all employees.

↘ Disneyland Paris Senior Manager Innovation, Audrey Mermet, is setting-up, a conference on intrapreneurship at his Tomorrow Lab, upfront to the launch of his program for intrapreneurs.

Interactions with applicants help to sort out the best potentials: it's not only a question of idea relevancy, it's a question of mindset, and both have to enrich each other. Intrapreneurs shall show that they are able to **listen and iterate**, **navigate and connect** within the group to find a sponsor or collect expertise, test their concept with users, and learn from it.

Starting from the outset the coaching of candidates is a guarantee to have the best upshot at the end of the program, and contributes more broadly to intrapreneurship acculturation.

⬃ Tilkee (a French startup in SaaS services) Founder, Sylvain Tillon, has a wise opinion on this. He believes that you're not intrinsically innovative simply because you're a startup: 'startup' doesn't always equate 'innovation'. Therefore, they have set-up an intrapreneurship device to yield innovation: **the Intrapreneurs Day**.

Every year, at the beginning of September, the entire team takes part in something called **'Startup Friday**'! The web developers present their ideas to the whole team and based on the best ideas, groups of salespeople and devs are formed. Each team works throughout the day to take the initial idea, and come up with a business model, landing page, and fully functioning prototype by 6pm. Each idea is then pitched, and demonstrated to the whole team.

It's a great day which encourages the web developers and sales teams to mingle, and work together. It's interesting for both groups to see the ins and outs of the work that the others do, and this is actually beneficial for the whole team all year long. Furthermore, Tilkee genuinely dedicates resources to each innovation, and does its best to take them to market: examples are Tilkee for Marketing, Foxy the connected fox, Tilkee for Events, Autolike, Copilot and SemanTilk which have all come out of 'Startup Friday'!

>> SELECTION

How Vinci, Orange, Trumpf, Telefonica do it

To sort out applications, most companies use a **jury** to select the projects that will go for incubation.

⌐ My Vinci Startup, the intrapreneurs' incubation program of Vinci, received almost 100 answers from their first Group-wide call, explains Matthieu Lerondeau, Head of Communications & Communities. A selection committee, including **external** partners, selected 10 of them, led by people from a large diversity of brands and trades in VINCI. The only instructions that they gave to applicants were to craft a new business value proposition, and to suggest new business ideas that would be **relevant to at least 2 brands** of VINCI.

⌐ Orange jury is composed of representatives from the business, and the countries where Orange operates, from the innovation and technology division, and from the open innovation and corporate venture teams. The **public vote** is collected during the pitch session in front of the jury, and an audience of 250 employees. Selection criteria include: clarity of the value proposition, market size and attractiveness, unfair advantage that Orange can bring, and credibility of the intrapreneur.

Credibility of the intrapreneur incorporates his passion and determination. It also considers his ability to attract resources on his project, and his potential as a team leader. **The team is what turns the dream into reality**, as it is developed in step 5.

All in all, while the project can be at an early stage at selection gate, with no proof of concept, it's the combination of a **clear problem / value proposition, the asset that the corporation can bring to the project, and the ascendency** of the intrapreneur that make a difference.

↘ Trumpf innovation ideas shall target markets that could be characterized as '**new technology in a new market, based on existing core competencies**' shares Ann-Sophie Reinelt Innovations Manager - Programmleitung Intrapreneur Programm.

↘ Telefonica runs **AI** across the projects candidates to cross-check, and complement its selection.

It is acute to look at the selection from a global point of view, and articulate an **innovation portfolio** strategy: some projects might be looking for quick wins while others aim at opening new business lines; how the variety of projects represents the geographical footprint of the company is also an input.

Following the jury selection, one shall think of those who have not been selected: an **after jury session** can cheer up unfortunate candidates. A process can be considered to examine ideas left behind, and see how some can be reused.

An **auto-intrapreneur kit** can help the idea owners who want to keep on enriching their project. Board of Innovation has developed an Innovation Virtual Consultant who takes the idea owner through 19 questions to improve his project.

>> INCUBATION PROCESS

How Vinci, Thales, Orange, Bosch, Telefonica do it

What is at stake now is to **phase the incubation, with tasks to achieve in a 3-4 months period, i.e. clear deadlines, and create a creative tension, an enticing rhythm** for the incubation stage.

⌲ Vinci selected intrapreneurs are offered 2 progressive steps:

- a **4-months journey,** during which they dedicate **20%** of their time pursuing their projects as well as receiving coaching, and mentoring from the Leonard team, experts and entrepreneurs who are ready to share their knowledge and experience;
- Then a new selection committee determines which projects will carry on their journey on an extra **full-time 4 months period** (100% time dedicated to the project).

⌲ Thales Digital Factory accelerates the digital transformation, by co-selecting innovation opportunities with the business lines, framing them, building MVPs, iterating, and refining along until the final transfer to the business line, explain Hamilton Mann, Group Director, Digital Marketing and Digital Transformation, Stéphane El Mabrouk, Head of Operations of the Digital Thales Factory, and Jean-Yves Plu Vice President, Digital Ecosystem.

Innovation tackles **new businesses**, as well as "**re-platforming**" existing service with digital. New growth projects might as well transition outside of business units. Though it is not limited to intrapreneurship, this well-structured and fast-track process is quite insightful:

1. Business Innovation, and Growth **Challenges** aim at embarking all the employees of the Group to turn experimentation into norm, identifying business problems to be solved, and bringing to life Proof of Concept, Proof of Value, and prototyping;
2. **Framing** takes place during **2 weeks** for most promising ideas: value proposition canvas and business model canvas are fulfilled upstream, and then confronted with the Business Units. Training is provided to lay the skills foundation; 5 workshops challenge are set-up to validate the business case solidity, and enter the next stage; 3 to 4 framing can be handled concurrently, involving 30 to 35 projects that will end into a selection of a dozen going for MVPs; other projects can be processed within the business units;

3. **MVPs are structured in cycle of 8 sprints going over 4 months**; 60% of the projects ask for a second cycle to refine the MVP, or complete the hand-over; MVP is business case oriented so as to test the business line commitment; this framework is designed for acceleration, with a **4 months deadline triggering a positive tension**.

Some programs go beyond MVP, down to the scale-up phase.

⬎ Bosch Startup Platform Grow Founder, Peter Guse (now New Business Development at VECTOR Informatik), defines it as a platform for startups, and an open space for entrepreneurs inside of Bosch. He structured a pyramid of 3 interactive formats:

1. **Safari, a half-day workshop** that is run on demand for up to 40 participants, mostly Bosch employees with or without idea, to explain what the offer is, and how lean startup works, what ideas they are looking for, and what is expected from the teams;
2. **Expedition** is run up to **4 times per year for 4-8 teams** with ideas. Within **2,5 days** they coach the teams with external and internal experts on how to structure the business model, interview customers, put a pitch and story together and present the case to a jury. From Expedition Bosch selects and invites the best teams for the next stage;

3. **Discovery** is the **lean accelerator** passed in part time **one day per week** parallel to the everyday job over **10 weeks**, again working intensely on the idea with experts, and aligning expectations for the final pitch to the board for incubation funding;

With funding granted, **1 or 2 teams per year are offered to join Grow** giving up the former job and moving with the other teams in the Grow location in Ludwigsburg. Scale up, and gradual transition to a business division over **1-2 years**, seems to work most promisingly.

↘ Orange intrapreneurs' incubation is structured according to 4 **lean startup pillars**:

1. **Problem/solution fit** in 3 months;
2. **MVP** (Minimum Viable Product, the minimum version of your product, with just enough features to enable valid user feedback): testing basic to advanced MVP from month 6 to 9;
3. **Product/market fit** (proving a significant number of sales or user acquisition and activations from your market target): from month 12 to 18;
4. **Getting ready for Scale-Up** from month 18 to 24.

↘ Telefonica **thorough roadmap** stands out as it is an instructive guide for intrapreneurs; this clear framework, truly helps intrapreneurs:

1. **Ideation**: Validating the customer target, the problem to solve, and the solution proposed in **3 months**.
2. **Prototype**: Development of a functional prototype based on customer interactions to achieve solution-product fit, from **6 to 9 additional months**.
3. **Beta**: Build a Minimum Marketable Product, and sell it to early customers, achieving product-market fit, between **12 months and 18 additional months**.
4. **Product**: Industrialize the product, and grow the customer base, from **9 to 12 additional months**.
5. **Scale-up**: Scale a profitable business, and usually transferring the product to a business unit. Limited to a maximum of **12 months**.

Another important aspect on which Telefonica has worked is **How to kill a project** in order to desacralize the fact to stop a project. When they kill a project (and this is something that might be even done by the intrapreneur himself/herself), 3 things happen: communicate to the whole organization the rationale for the decision, and recognize the team for their work, relocate people in other projects, and do a debriefing session to extract the learnings so the team can see their effort has brought value to the company.

Killing a project is a delicate matter, but it is much better than putting it on a drip, on hold or leaving into coma.

⌟ Gore example of the **Celebrate Failure** party is famous: "Celebrate failure, don't stigmatize it. When a project doesn't work out and the team kills it, they celebrate with beer or champagne just as if it had cut the mustard! Celebrating a failure encourages risk taking. It's also perfect timing for project leaders to see which resources are now available! "

⌟ Intrapreneur Nation Consulting Firm has drafted a **Corporate Entrepreneurship Roadmap** involving 9 steps:

1. **Vision and Team**: Cross-functional team, and big, hairy, audacious goals;
2. **Market and Customer**: Segment the market. Zoom in on the early adopters;
3. **Problems and Opportunities**: Gain deep insights into customer tasks, pains, challenges, goals and values;
4. **Sketch**: Sketch your solution. Get rapid, structured feedback from the target market;
5. **Value Proposition**: Develop, and validate your core marketing messages;
6. **Channels, Revenues, and Costs**: Develop the financial and distribution models;
7. **MVP and Soft launch**: Focus on learning not selling. Possibly get your first paying customers;
8. **Innovation Accounting**: Track the leading metrics that are predictors of growth;
9. **Growth experiments**: Systematically develop and launch experiments to shift the dial on growth;

→ Then **Learn, Pivot or Scale.**

Intrapreneur Nation advices to wait for customers' feedback before formulating the value proposition in step 5: "This is why you should develop the value proposition after you've validated your solution sketch with prospects" told me Intrapreneur Nation.

Don't get overwhelmed by the diverse incubation processes presented! Whether it's in-depth incubation like in Telefonica, or in short sprints like in Vinci and Thalès, the common cornerstone is to **focus the bulk of time in relentlessly testing the intrapreneur concept with the user target**, and chase regular insights: that is the notion behind the MVP. Once the first test completed, life must become **innovation in short cycles** for the intrapreneur: **develop, test, learn, rachet-up, and iterate.**

As intrapreneurs are not always innovation specialist, a **Welcome Kit,** describing the phasing of the program, and the expected deliverables every 3 to 4 months, will be very appreciated.

Reversely, at the end of incubation, it makes perfect sense to organize a **Demo Day** where intrapreneurs can present their achievements, and celebrate together successes and learnings ("I never fail, either I succeed, either I learn" as Mandela puts it), and meet again with those who were at the initial jury selection event.

>> LOCAL OR CENTRALIZED INCUBATION

How Orange, LVMH, Continental, Nissan, Red-Cross do it

Incubation can be localized or centralized.

↘ Orange has trained a network of 30 **intrapreneurs' boosters** worldwide. Their tasks are to:

- Inspire & reassure, raising interest in intrapreneurship;
- Support ideation & applications;
- Facilitate business unit sponsors endorsement, and collaboration;
- Support local incubation: boosters have the ability to **coach an intrapreneur locally**, and help him set-up his team, and organize his work.

As applications come from over a dozen countries in the world, it made sense for Orange to build this **local innovation capability**.

↘ LVMH rolls out his DARE acceleration days (2 days workshop to move an idea to a business plan) from Paris to Shanghai, and entices 60 employees from Asia Pacific region in intrapreneurship.

↘ Continental runs 4-months incubation taking place in Mexico City, Chongqing, and in Berlin. The previous year, the program was available in Munich in which teams from ten different countries could participate, explains Jürgen Bilo, Managing Director / Vice President of Co-pace, the organization of Continental to incubate startups, and intrapreneurs.

↘ Nissan, BNP Paribas, French Red-Cross organize innovation sessions where all intrapreneurs meet in the same place. This is definitely more impactful for the cohort spirit, fostering an intrapreneurs class grade, and easier to settle. But travels organization is cumbersome in the long run, the intrapreneur lacks support once back to his desk, and it misses the local transformation goal.

KEY QUESTIONS

This series of questions helps you to define the most efficient process:

>> PROCESS

- What are the main steps of the identification / selection / incubation stages?
- What are the selection criteria? How do they stick to business expectations? Will you look mainly for business innovation for outside market, or also for internal process optimization?
- What are the expected output and outcome of the incubation? An advanced MVP, a product market-fit, or a product that is ready to scale? What are the

timeline for the various stages of incubation? What are the deadlines and deliverables expected?

- What is the board to review these items? Will you apply Stage Gate process / Go No Go reviews?
- What is the process to stop a project?
- How will you handle incubation, centrally or locally?

>> COMMUNICATION

- What are the channels (events, internal social network, intranet, newsletter …), and the spokesmen to promote the program?
- Is a network of boosters / catalysts necessary to act as local intrapreneurship referents?
- What is the toolbox to support marketing and communication of the program for intrapreneurs to the different targets: intrapreneurs, managers, business units?
- How to ensure regular communication about the projects and the intrapreneurs, keeping the various audiences informed (intrapreneurs, employees, managers, sponsors, business units, HR, innovation managers)?
- How to avoid overvaluing intrapreneurs vs other employees, keeping them humble, and connected with the workforce?

MAIN RISK

Fuzziness doesn't help innovation. The main risk is not be clear enough on expectations and speed of the incubation, and let the initial energy dilute and timeline extend, instead of **keeping a creative tension** with sprints clearly focused on catering to customer needs.

Step 5: Intrapreneurs status, coaching, and resources

CHALLENGE

This is another one of the top-3 challenges, and it's not a duck soup. It is to define the **time allocation** of the intrapreneur, and the **coaching and resources** that will be provided.

Since the intrapreneur has been selected in step 4, he has not suddenly turned into a seasoned entrepreneur and innovation project leader: providing him with the appropriate coaching is paramount.

USE CASES

>> TIME ALLOCATION, AND STATUS

How Vinci, La Poste, Air France, Accor, Spring Lab, Airbus do it

Time allocation can vary according to the progression of the idea. Once the project is on tracks, and has passed some validation gates, it is recommended to provide a full time allocation: why would the intrapreneur succeed part-time when entrepreneur need full-time?

⟱ Vinci intrapreneurs are firstly offered a 4-months journey, **20% of their time** dedicated to pursuing their projects, and then an extra full-time 4 months period (**100% time** dedicated to the project).

⟱ La Poste (French Mail Company) intrapreneurs are allocated 100% for 12 months on their project, with a Go / No Go review every 3 months.

⟱ Air France happened to allocate time to the intrapreneur team so that the totality of time allocated to the different team members equates one full time job.

⟱ AccorHotels offers intrapreneurs a **6-week incubation phase at 50% of their time** in the Techstars incubator, during which they can test their project, and measure its viability, explains Laurence Bordry VP Innovation Lab Marketing Global at AccorHotels.

But smaller companies might be constrained in terms of time allocation.

⟱ Spring Lab is an innovation agency instilling startups mindset into large corporations:

- Because they believe that good employees are inspired and proud employees, they have built intrapreneurship program that cultivates entrepreneurship among employees, explains Heloise Lauret, one of Spring-Lab co-founders;

- Spring Lab grants **6 days off** employee's annual work time to engage in a project that makes sense, and is compliant with clear criteria:
    - The project has an accurate scope;
    - It has a link with core activities: creativity, startups, digital;
    - It entices the use of employee professional skills;
    - It takes no longer than 6 days per year, and day off will be notified as soon as possible.
- It "means a lot" to employees, it forces them to go a little bit out of their comfort zone, and they take a lot of pleasure in doing it!

The intrapreneur can remain linked to his original unit (no impact on his contract and payroll): then a **letter of mission** specifies the length of the mission, and the project he will be working on.

A **special evaluation** of intrapreneur performance has to be handled, considering his change of position. It will involve the stakeholders of his project (business unit sponsor, incubation team).

A **dedicated HR contact** for the intrapreneur will be identified, and support him in his new role.

⬂ Airbus is preparing an intrapreneur status, corresponding to a **quality mark**, and a processing box with a way in, and a way out. Actually, intrapreneurs don't stay attached to their initial unit: their manager is free to replace them, and this is a **risk** the intrapreneur has to face. At the end of incubation, intrapreneur can come back to his manager, and try to convince him to hire him back, or he can look for another position.

To clarify the mutual engagements of the company and the intrapreneur, **a chart of engagements** can be signed by both parties.

↘ Make sense incubator has drafted a very accurate model summarizing objectives, state of mind, roles and responsibilities, and practical aspects: http://bit.ly/CHARTEINTRA.

>> COACH'S ROLE

How Orange, Total, Ministry of the Armed Forces do it

Because many intrapreneurs have no experience in innovation project management, or venture creation, **tailored coaching is of the utmost importance** on the following dimensions:

- Keeping **intrapreneur mood** elated: setbacks are harsh, and leading the project can be grueling;
- Ensuring **team cohesion**;

- Explaining the **innovation path**, in consistency with the incubation process, and keeping the creative tension;
- Helping the intrapreneur to **connect to allies**, and attract resources.

⅃ Orange has trained intrapreneurs' boosters at the coach's role, and drafted a **short guide** for a coaching session between an intrapreneur, and his coach:

Intrapreneur State of Mind

- How do you feel?
- Do you feel at ease at your intrapreneur's mission (on a scale from 1 to 10)? Why?
- What kind of support or skill would you need?

Team

- Regarding team cohesion and consistency, on a scale from 1 to 10, what would be the rate? Why?
- What can eventually be lacking in the team, any staffing issue? What's holding you back?
- Describe team meetings. When is your next team workshop?

Project (innovation path)

- Which hypotheses were tested since our last meeting?

- What did you learn on the project? What do the users/clients say?
- What are our learnings for our next tests, and the business model canvas update?

Network of Allies

- How would you describe your relationship with the BU sponsor?
- How are the roles distributed with the BU sponsor?
- What new contacts could be developed, and stakeholders contacted?

Next steps

- What are the 3 points you would like to work on before our next appointment?
- When is your next project board? How would you like to prepare it?
- How much better do you feel after this session? And regarding your project?

↘ Total Head of Business Acceleration, Claire Le Louët, explains how coaching is provided by its startups studio to accelerate selected intrapreneurs:

- Intrapreneurs first move from enrolment (1 month), to new business design (3 months), and final pitch in front of a jury with a 20% time allocation;

- Then the startups studio carries on **continuous coaching with internal board of advisors, and 3 to 4 specialized consultants full-time,** bringing intrapreneurs through new offer design and market traction (3 months), business model validation, prototyping & field testing (6 months to 1 year), go-to-market strategy, and scalability (1 year) with a 100% time allocation, and a business line mandate.

Total has drafted an **intrapreneur kit** with 10 data sheets related to NDA (non-disclosure agreement), collaboration with startups, intrapreneur behavior ...

↘ French Ministry of the Armed Forces handles a mission for participatory innovation: it has coached 70 projects per year for 30 years with **financial and technical support**, explains Thibault Perrin, Mission Leader for Intrapreneurship, at the Innovation Defense Agency.

>> INTRAPRENEUR MINDSET

How Amazon, Lego, Total, Airbus do it

Intrapreneurs are often **scrappy** and born-determined people: coaching shall help them to acquire flexibility, drive them to this **ability to listen, and iterate**.

↘ Amazon Founder Jeff Bezos shares that being a mind-boggling entrepreneur requires to be both **stubborn and flexible**.

Likewise, intrapreneur shall balance the large autonomy he receives, with a solid sense of responsibility: intrapreneurship implies accountability.

Coach can help the intrapreneur **navigate within the group, and develop a network of allies**.

⌄ Lego Brand Group Intrapreneur in Residence, David Gram, speaks of **diplomatic rebels**: intrapreneurs need to balance the curiosity and resilience of the rebel, whilst channeling the humble, listening diplomat.

Fleeing shallowness, intrapreneur has the relentless capacity to test his idea and hypotheses (never mistake a wish for a certainty!), capture insights, as well as to connect, and attract resources. **Intrapreneur quells ignorance with resilience, and cultivates grace**.

⌄ Total intrapreneur **psychology** gives birth to a variety of situations: some don't want to let go of their project while others are willing to transfer, some have difficulties to reinforce the skills of the team.

⌄ Airbus Acceleration Program Manager & Startups x Intrapreneurs Coach (at Madrid incubator BizLab), Soraya Ferahtia, stresses on the **frugal and makers** dimensions of intrapreneurship, during the 6 months of incubation. She believes the perfect program is the one which adapts to each personality, with close **one-to-one coaching**. Nevertheless Airbus is looking for **autonomous and self-starter**

intrapreneurs, as well as collective players: intrapreneurs' projects are presented by a team of 2 people, one will be full time, and the other one at 20% time allocation.

>> COACHING RESOURCES, AND INTRAPRENEURS' MIXING

How Orange, Société Générale, La Poste, Airbus, Nexity do it

Coaching can be delivered on an **individual basis, as well as collectively**, completing team workshop to outstrip milestones: building the vision, validating the problem/solution fit, designing the MVP, updating the value proposition and the BMC, achieving product/market fit.

External **mentors,** like seasoned entrepreneurs, can bring an entrepreneur point of view to the intrapreneur.

The **Intrapreneurs Marketplace**, initiated by Gefco and Orange, helps intrapreneurs connect with other intrapreneurs, and with corporate intrapreneurship managers, to gain feedback on their projects.

Coaching can be **internalized** like with Orange boosters, and completed with **external** incubators like at Engie, La Poste, and Société Générale.

- Renowned intrapreneurs' incubators are makesense, School Lab, Numa, Paris&Co, Station F, Techstars France, in France, or The do school in Germany;

- Other innovation agencies offer intrapreneurs support without hosting them: Epigo (with their soulful purpose "allow everyone to connect with his power to act" inspired by Spinoza), Create Rocks, Corporate for Change, Fly the Nest, Spring Lab, Change Factory, Inskip, YA+K, Start the f up, Startup inside in France, Board of Innovation in Belgium,... As well as innovation coaches like Olivier Schwartz and Fabien Canitrot.

↘ External incubations feed intrapreneurs with fresh air, and connections with co-located startups. This is exactly what highlights Paris & Co, the incubator of Paris region: **mixing intrapreneurs with entrepreneurs** in the same place.

↘ Airbus and Nexity co-locate intrapreneurs with startups in their corporate accelerator. Nexity actually pushes the envelope a bit further: they share program for startups and intrapreneurs according to the following schedule:

- 1 week of boot camp;
- 3 months market hook;
- 1 to 6 months for market test.

Naturally, the flip side of hosting intrapreneurs in a separate location is that it creates a gap between the intrapreneur, and the core company business units.

Nevertheless, external incubators are utterly precious when there is no innovation space, and innovation expert resources at the home entity of the intrapreneur.

The first mix to create is obviously the **intrapreneurs' community**: making intrapreneurs meet, to share experience, imagine, co-build, is highly beneficial. Intrapreneurs look to be challenged, to work their pitch, finding teammates, skills and ultimately to be recognized.

Last but not least, when internal resources are used, and coaching relies on **volunteer coaches**, one must have in mind **coaches' consideration** so that they become resilient resources.

>> TEAM BUILDING

A particularly tricky point is the team building:

- More and more, intrapreneur is actually **a couple of intrapreneurs**: it is the beginning of a team, and it represents a more balanced strength than a sole intrapreneur;
- Intrapreneurs can be encouraged to look for team members, as a test for their capacity to convince, and embark on their idea; **contributors** can also be searched via a request for contributions on the company social network; status and reward for contributors have to be described, taking also into

account the impact on managers who are giving resources away.

- The spirit of the team is a delicate matter, ensuring that all contributors share the vision, letting them act with autonomy, develop their co-leadership because they see it as their own the project as well: then you can have 'a whole greater than the sum of the parts'.

An innovation team works like a business unit. You're all working towards a common goal, but everyone also has their own plan.

>> TEAM RESOURCES, AND BUDGET

How La Poste, Trumpf, Orange, Telefonica do it

Resources and budget can be allocated at the start of the incubation, or according to the project progression, and the gates it passes.

↘ La Poste dedicates a **standard** envelope for external purchase (staffing of digital expertise) per project, tells us former Intrapreneurship Program Manager, Carmen Rouanet.

↘ Trumpf distinctive feature is that **all funding is made available to the intrapreneurs' teams right at the start, and fully at their discretion**. In practical terms, every team is provided with a dedicated bank account which is filled with necessary funding. The teams can decide on their own on how to spend the budget as they advance to demonstrate problem/solution-fit, product/market-fit via Minimum Viable Products, and viability of the business model.

⊻ Orange **tailors** internal human resources (designer, coder, product marketer, business developer) and in addition, budget to external staffing, according to project needs, and progression.

⊻ Telefonica manages innovation projects through stage-gates, and a metered funding approach, where **incremental funding is conditional on the project's results**, in order to minimize the risk of the bets;

Resources have to be reshuffled depending on progression:

- At an early stage, a **User Experience Designer** is required to validate problem / solution fit, help structure and conduct user interviews, and questionnaires, and design the resulting customer experience; tools involved are: value proposition canvas, persona, observation and interviews, mock-up; **Product Marketing** skills contribute to build the vision of the product, complete benchmark, competitive analysis, and business model canvas; **Technical** feasibility, and rough digital architecture are achieved if the service has a prominent digital dimension; depending on his background, the intrapreneur can take the product marketing or the CTO (Chief Technical Officer) hat; it is not recommended for the intrapreneur to take the UX role, as it might introduce a bias in garnering customer insights;

- At the next stage, globally corresponding to MVP and testing assumptions, **User Interface Designer** and Product Marketing will take a larger role; customer journey design, web landing page, MVP building, tests, and pilots are the main tasks to achieve;
- Partnerships, and sales might involve also an **Innovation Business Developer**, who will be even more committed in the next stage of reaching product/market fit, and scale-up preparation;
- **Finance** will take in charge the business plan for scale-up, while **Digital Marketing** will contribute to product/market fit with online campaigns (social media), growth hacking, and trade shows (BtoB).

>> FACILITATION, AND PROGRAM MANAGEMENT

How Vinci, Nissan do it

To design, and handle the Intrapreneurship program, and build a **positive ecosystem** for the intrapreneurs, a **small dedicated facilitation team** is necessary.

It includes marketing and community management skills for the identification phase, innovation / entrepreneurial, coaching, HR, business competencies for the selection and incubation phases. And all dimensions are to be considered for an accurate design of the program as we see in this guide! Navigation within the company to catch program recognition by managers is mandatory.

⌄ Leonard, Vinci Innovation Lab, is run by a dedicated team of **6 people** from diverse backgrounds:

1. Chief Leonard Officer, with an entrepreneur background;
2. Head of Innovative Projects and Intrapreneurship, with a long history with Vinci;
3. Head of Operations and Foresight;
4. Head of Communities and Communications, run by an entrepreneur for 10 years in the digital communication and innovation agency;
5. Head of Acceleration, led by a former Senior Associate at BNP Paribas in San Francisco and a scholar;
6. Communication Manager working on communications and community management, reporting to the Head of Communities and Communications.

⌄ Nissan Innovation Lab for Europe is a team of 10 people, but only **3 manage the corporate entrepreneur program**, the other 7 act as business developers on 7 thematic verticals for future business involving the business units, explains Ivan Ollivier, Director Nissan Europe Innovation Lab.

The more the facilitation of the program for intrapreneurs is supported by **external incubation partners**, the less numerous is the internal program management team.

Taking into account the various dimensions of program for intrapreneurs, one must look for **a senior manager to handle the program**. His sets of prowess include team management / HR / coaching, program design, innovation methodology, and business strategy.

⬎ Amélie Moutiers, student at Paris University, suggests in her bright dissertation about programs for intrapreneurs management, that upfront training might be very relevant for nominee, as well as an entrepreneurial immersion for one month.

>> ALUMNI

And when it's finished? Well intrapreneurship is never over!

A network of former intrapreneurs is useful to keep these "agent of change" postures alive, reconnect them with their peers, and recharge their batteries. They can also contribute to internal and external communication (toward future employees), recruitment of intrapreneurs, or coaching of new projects.

KEY QUESTIONS

This series of questions helps you to define status, coaching, and resources' allocation:

- Will the time allocation vary according to the progression of the intrapreneurs across Identification, selection, and incubation stages?
- What will be the impact on his status? Will a letter of mission clarify his role?
- What kind of coaching will be set-up, at which frequency, and who will handle it? Will it reach out for external resources?
- What amount of resources/budget will be allocated, depending on which objectives, and achievements?
- What are the skills staffed to help the intrapreneur at the successive stages of the project?
- Who is the team who will manage the intrapreneurship approach from A to Z?
- How will it be structured, and rewarded? What is planned for them after the program?

MAIN RISK

One substantial risk is to underestimate the role of coaching, and **consider that fledgling intrapreneurs are born-innovation projects managers**. Insufficient guidance can result in intrapreneur being focused on his solution, and not on the customer's problem: "Love the problem, not your solution" underlines Ash Maurya, creator of the Lean Canvas, author of renowned innovation books Running Lean, and Scaling Lean, and of the preface of this book!

Innovation is a discipline, it takes some time, and guidance to acquire it: coaching supports this, and their role shall be recognized, and rewarded, especially when the contribution is voluntary.

Step 6: Business units commitment

This is our third of the top-3 challenges: onboarding business units in the program from the outset, turning them from passive bystanders to **active stakeholders**.

One will not become an active stakeholder because you will sell him your innovative idea: business units commit when innovation solves a **problem** for them, or create a business **opportunity**: this is what the intrapreneur has to look for.

USE CASES

>> LINKING WITH BUSINESS UNITS

How Deutsche Bahn, Thales, Nissan, Total, AccorHotels do it

↘ Deutsche Bahn program, DB Intrapreneurs, works hand-in-hand with all business units across silos: interdisciplinarity and co-creation are paramount to innovate within a corporate. Henceforth, **business units can bring their own project to the program**.

↘ Thales Digital Factory accelerates the Digital Transformation, by **co-selecting innovation opportunities with the business lines**, framing them, building MVPs, iterating, and refining along until the final transfer to the business line, explains Stéphane El Mabrouk, Head of Operations of the Digital Thales Factory.

↘ Nissan Innovation Lab has spotted 7 thematic verticals (for instance, factory 4.0): each vertical covers one or several business units. Business units involved can send **one intrapreneur per vertical** to be incubated at the Lab. Ceding entity keeps paying him: he will work on a topic that matters to them, **they are committed from the start**.

Nevertheless, if intrapreneurship purpose (identified in step 1) is to embark all employees, then intrapreneurs will look up for **sponsoring business unit beyond the entity** they are currently working in.

During the project incubation, business units can help with **funding**.

↘ Total business units can take over on the budget at any time: at the end of phase 1 (new offer design, and market traction), phase 2 (business model validation, prototyping, and field testing), or phase 3 (go-to-market strategy, and scalability).

↘ AccorHotels asks for a different contribution: **the payroll of the intrapreneur is recharged to the BU sponsor** by the ceding entity; with this money, the manager can hire a consultant to handle the work the intrapreneur has left away.

Business units can open doors for market tests, and pilots, and arrange their product line for the intrapreneurs offering. Some sharp expertise like legal might also be very precious, for instance when the intrapreneur project involves cooperation with a startup.

>> CONVINCING A BU SPONSOR

How Orange, Engie, La Poste do it

↘ Orange has drafted a leaflet, listing benefits that an intrapreneur can bring to a business unit to onboard it as a **sponsor**, which is mandatory for their selection stage.

1. **Business opportunity**: explain what opportunity creates your innovation for your target Business Unit (BU) sponsor; does it bring market differentiation, communication opportunity, churn reduction, additional revenue line, new customers, process optimization and cost reduction...?
2. **Progressive commitment**: the BU sponsor investment is about time and expertise, it is progressive along with the business for the BU;
3. **Being part of the intrapreneurs project**: the BU sponsor can allocate a specific resource to the intrapreneur project;

4. **Acceleration**: the BU sponsor can take advantage of the intrapreneurship and the Intrapreneurs Studio incubation to give life to an idea born in its business unit;

5. **Active monitoring**: stakeholders (BU sponsor / region or country) are part of project reviews, where the interest of all the parties is protected, and valued; involved upstream, BU sponsor can anticipate hand-over at the end of the incubation;

6. **Cross-BUs collaboration**: the BU sponsor can use intrapreneurship to push a project that involves several BUs;

7. **Culture and Objectives**: the BU sponsor will observe empowerment of employees through intrapreneurship, and nimble innovation, which can infuse the business unit culture; the intrapreneur project will contribute to the innovation objectives of the BU sponsor / manager;

8. **Company attractiveness**: allowing innovative employees to pursue their creative projects for the benefit of the company and its customers will increase company's attractiveness as an employer's brand; it will offer new talents a field of creativity and professional development;

9. **Customer proximity**: the BU, with its operational objectives, will demonstrate its proximity to the field,

with the customer experience at the heart of the innovation project;

10. **Proven track-record**: the BU will capitalize on a selection, and incubation process that has managed successful exits for intrapreneurs' projects, thanks to close coaching and the sponsor BU, and intrapreneurs' determination!

↘ Engie (French Energy Company) requires each intrapreneur to **hook a BU sponsor** as well, details Emmanuel France, New Business Incubation Director for 3 years. As a result, 3 of their first intrapreneur projects have landed in business units.

↘ La Poste (French Mail Company) has worked on a model where the **intrapreneur is hosted by the sponsoring business unit** after 3 months of incubation.

To pave the way for intrapreneurs looking for Business units Sponsors, the intrapreneurship team should go on road-show, **onboarding the business units upstream** in the approach, setting-up one to one meeting, and leveraging the relay of the Ambassadors / Boosters network.

One challenge is also to accommodate business units to small business streams of several hundred of k€, which corresponds to intrapreneurs' projects revenues initially: one way is to invite **external entrepreneurs at the intrapreneurs'**

steering committee as they are familiar with these small starts.

KEY QUESTIONS

These questions help you to enroll a business sponsor.

>> BUSINESS ALIGNMENT

- What are the current issues that the business units are facing? Competition, digitalization, necessity to innovate, employees' spirits, flawed processes...?
- How can intrapreneurship create opportunities for them, and solve problems?
- How will the business priorities / issues be incorporated? During the request for ideas, in the selection criteria, and composition of the jury?
- How can the business units engage during incubation? Allocating resources, opening customer channel for field test, participating in project board...

MAIN RISK

One substantial risk is to **involve the business units too late, jeopardizing the further landing and scaling at the business unit**, or to disengage them later in the process, by not integrating their feedback. Remember entrepreneurs can be stubborn as Jeff Bezos says... An intrapreneur has two customers or stakeholders: the business unit sponsor and the end customer.

Step 7: Exit scenarios, innovation business development, and scale-up

CHALLENGE

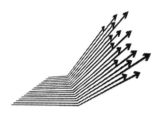

Exit scenarios for the projects and the intrapreneurs have to be designed upstream; then, when the end of incubation is near, you will assess them, and select the best one.

A **business development dedicated to innovation** might be crucial to accelerate the exit, and **hand-over** to a business unit, or metamorphosis into a startup.

USE CASES

>> EXIT SCENARIOS

How La Poste, Orange, Total, Trumpf do it

4 exit scenarios arise frequently:

1. The intrapreneur project lands to a business unit or corporate functions; it can become a business unit itself;
2. The intrapreneur project is handled through a dedicated scaling-up unit in the core company;

3. The intrapreneur project turns into a separate legal entity, created by the company with majority shares (subsidiary); minority shares can be allocated to the intrapreneur at preferred rate, according to his contribution, and to future business achievements (Equity / BSPCE for intrapreneurs);
4. The intrapreneur project turns into an external legal entity created by the intrapreneur (spin-off / spin-out into a startup, with minority shares for the group or no share at all); preferred shares and priority dividend, along with precise reporting, can be negotiated by the company with the intrapreneur, in the valuation of intellectual property; BSA Ratchet allow preferred rate for the next fundraising, BSA Relution are used in case of failure.

↘ Bosch Startup Platform welcomes 1 or 2 teams per year, with funding granted, giving up the former job, and moving in the Grow location in Ludwigsburg. Scale up, and gradual transition to a business division takes over 1-2 years. Grow acts as **a dedicated scaling-up unit** in the core company.

Scenarios can embed employee **intellectual property** valorization, depending on the intellectual property company rule. Scenarios 3 and 4 can drive **shares split** with the intrapreneur.

↘ La Poste (French Mail Company) has designed and tested 2 main exit scenarios:

1. **Subsidiary set-up**: an investment committee takes the decision after one year incubation; intrapreneurs become the corporate officer (social representative) with a mobility contract that secures the possibility to come back, over a 4 years period, a guaranteed salary, and 5% to 20% shares depending on results achieved;

2. **Spin off**: the intrapreneur is no more in the headcount; the investment during the incubation is valuated through the level of shares of the startup for the core company (typically around 20% shares of the startup), and the value of the shares resulting from fundraising: for instance, if fundraising show that 20% shares correspond to 250 k€; then the core company can take 20%, by evaluating its incubation to 200 k€, and bringing an additional 50 k€.

⅃ Orange crosses different points of view to elaborate exit scenarios:

<u>Exit scenarios from a project point of view</u>

- Hand-over to BUs;
- New business line;
- Extrapreneurship, intrapreneur turning into entrepreneur;
- Sell-out / Outcubation;
- Stop.

75

The safeguards to ensure a fruitful exit are: BU sponsorship; jury support, and quarterly project board; embedding API in the product, for reuse and distribution; demo day.

From the intrapreneur point of view

- **Going along with the project, in or out of the core company**; there are some key indicators that the intrapreneur shall monitor to head toward the best scenario: product / market fit, quality of BU sponsor relationship, investment required for the scale-up, achievement of the scale-up canvas, time spent in incubation, …
- **Internal mobility with HR support, or going back to initial work entity**;
- **In all cases, skills development 'intrapreneurs certificate' with HEC (French Business School)**.

From an HR point of view

- Tailor-made process to support intrapreneur next step: one to one meeting to elaborate next steps scenarios with intrapreneur's coach; meeting prepared with Intrapreneurs Studio's team.
- Potential scenarios: Intrapreneur follows his project in BU, or takes the lead of the business line; intrapreneur goes back in his former unit; intrapreneur moves to entrepreneur;
- Celebrate failure, and success!

⊾ Total has completed several exits, from subsidiary (Total remains shareholder), to hand-over to business line.

Recognition of the individual's career, personal development, and learnings are key elements taken into account when the intrapreneur goes back to its former entity.

⊾ Trumpf intrapreneurship program, 'Internehmertum', was initially an initiative of the Corporate Technology and Innovation Management. Soon, it gained support from HR Development, and is becoming **an internal career building-block** in the future.

>> INNOVATION BUSINESS DEVELOPMENT

How Nissan, Mann + Hummel, Nexity do it

The engagement part where you confront your probe or MVP with users, and look up for business units that will distribute your service, is often underestimated. You might have the best product in the world, no salesman means no business!

For this time phase, innovation business development skills are a must-have.

What is an **Innovation Business Developer**?

- Tightly linked to the core product team, he can share the vision on the product, and be aware of the latest product roadmap: he's the soul mate of the product owner;

- He works on testing, and enriching the Value Proposition with target users, and shape a Unique Selling Proposition that fix user problems;
- He builds a network of contacts at Business Units or Partners that will help commercialize the product; he attracts support because he finds out how the innovative product can be a business opportunity for them.

In a nutshell, an Innovation Business Developer acts the same way a startup does: he explores new markets whose need will be catered by the new service, reaches out to contacts in this market that are open to innovative products, like Development Managers or Chief Innovation Officers, and unleashes **a channel for innovation**.

You might say I'm a dreamer, and that this role doesn't exist in real life? Take a look at the story of I2M.

↘ I2M stands for Innovation to Market: it is a **corporate venturing startup responsible for the commercialization of innovations** developed by Mann + Hummel research teams. Mann+Hummel is one of the world leaders in the filtration industry.

I2M mission consists in investigating new territories, and capturing business opportunities. Their focus areas are Clean

Air, Clean Water, Life Science and Energy. I2M is dedicated to the **business acceleration** stage of the innovation funnel, moving from incubation phase to sales.

Simple, fast, and effective are key values at I2M, who wants to behave like a startup, and aims to be a '0 fix cost' company. Charles Vaillant, EVP Technology at Mann+Hummel, and President & General Manager at I2M, sees "**the Innovation Business Developer as someone who behaves like a founder**, and has the same focus and determination".

⌐ Nissan Innovation Lab has formalized 4 scenarios to streamline proof of concept (POC) transition into business:

1. new business unit;
2. hand-over to existing business unit;
3. support from the transformation business unit;
4. and spin-out into a startup.

Transformation business unit is a dedicated entity which focuses on transitioning innovation into business. Each intrapreneur who joins this unit receives in addition the help of a Senior VP from the target business unit.

⌐ Nexity underscores a different device: to boost sales, intrapreneurs and startups have **a correspondent in each sales team** that the Startups Studio incentivizes for distributing the MVP. Correspondents are also put in visibility.

>> SCALE-UP CANVAS FOR INTRAPRENEURS

While there are many methodologies to start an innovation project (design thinking, lean startup, business model canvas, blue ocean,…) or to grow a proven business, there seems to be less support for the scale-up phase which comes after incubation.

Corporate scale-up have actually simultaneously to win a market, and to convince internally the corporation: the relationship between the new business, and the traditional one is a tricky topic that needs special focus.

↘ A group of corporate innovations practitioners, representing 10 premier European companies across various industries, the Scaling-Up Peer Group, has rounded up to address this scale-up chasm, facilitated by Frank Mattes and Ralph-Christian Ohr from Innovation 3, and produced a compelling book, Scaling-up Corporate Startups.

↘ Orange has created a **synthetic view** of the scale-up book, an operative tool at the hand intrapreneurs. The **Scale-Up Canvas** was tested, and iterated with Orange intrapreneurs.

It uses the Business Model Canvas to review 4 main thematic:

1. **Updating the value proposition** (Minimum Marketable Product) **and crossing the chasm**, corresponding to squares value proposition, and customers segments;

2. **Industrializing the product / service / business / supply processes**, corresponding to squares channels, customer relationships, activities, resources, and partners;

3. **Grooming the human organization for scale-up** (Minimum Scalable Venture), corresponding to squares resources;

4. **Transitioning the startup Management System to a Business Management System** corresponding to squares activities, revenues, and costs.

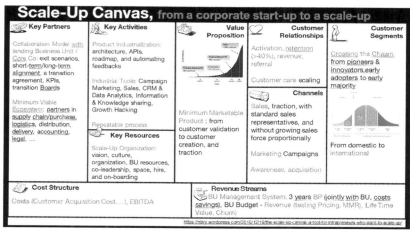

(Source: https://buff.ly/2Lo9tyk)

KEY QUESTIONS

An intrapreneur willing to scale should have these questions on his radar:

81

>> EXIT SCENARIOS

- What is the base case scenario among the 4 typical exit scenarios listed for the project? What are the best/worst scenarios?
- What is the preferred scenario for the intrapreneur? What is the plan B for the intrapreneur?

>> VALUE PROPOSITION, AND CROSSING THE CHASM

- Have you validated the MVP (Minimum Viable Product) and demonstrated product / market fit, tweaking the product to reach stability, and gain a significant number of customers?
- Have you designed a MMP (Minimum Marketable Product), a more advanced release of the MVP that present features, customer experience and look & feel (Minimum Lovable Product) to move from Trend Setters and Pioneers, Innovators, and Early Adopters to Early Majority? MMP is also when your business starts to get more awareness from the sponsoring business unit, and you enter a risk-mitigated stage;
- Have you addressed the relevance of extending this target market from domestic to international?

>> INDUSTRIALIZING PROCESSES

- Have you designed a growth plan, where growing Sales, and demonstrating traction (incoming flow of repeat business), with standard sales representatives (meaning without the personal involvement of the intrapreneur founder), do not entail growing sales force proportionally?

- Have you prepared Customer Care organization? You now have more and more customers, you will have after-sales request, you need to set-up a corresponding professional service;
- Have you started Product industrialization, going from a prototype to a robust Architecture? Preparing the ground for cooperation with the corporation IT with appropriate APIs? Sharing Product Roadmap, and automating Customer Feedbacks in an industrialized process?
- Have you implemented Industrial Tools to handle Campaign Marketing, Sales, CRM & Data Analytics, Information & Knowledge sharing, Growth Hacking techniques?
- Can you produce Business Metrics easily: awareness, acquisition, activation, retention, revenue, and referral?
- Are you upgrading your Minimum Viable Ecosystem (identified delivery partners, stabilizing organization and process related to supply chain/purchase, logistics, distribution, delivery, accounting, legal ...)?
- Overall, is your organization using Repeatable, still Agile Process, and is the Go for Scaling-up formalized, and agreed by all stakeholders?

>> TIGHTENING THE HUMAN ORGANIZATION

- Are you grooming the Scale-up Organization: vision, culture, core team for scaling-up, missions, governance, CEO co-leadership with CxO, locations, people hire to complement the core-team, and on-boarding of new hires?

>> TRANSITIONING TO A BUSINESS UNIT SYSTEM

- Have you implemented a Corporation Collaboration Model: value equation (what's in it for corporate startup and for the core), short-term/long-term strategic alignment, landing-spot, transition agreement, KPIs, and quarterly Transition Boards?
- Are you moving from Startup Management System to Business Unit Management System? Completing a 3 years Business Plan (jointly with the sponsoring business unit, including costs savings, and making the pathway-to-profitability apparent), matching with business unit Budget?
- Are you producing Business Metrics in an automated dashboard: Revenue (testing pricing, MMR - Monthly Recurring Revenue), recurrence (Lifetime Value, Churn), and Costs (Customer Acquisition Cost ...), EBITDA?
- When exiting to a startup, the collaboration model shall include VCs in the loop. Also the cash burn will become a vital issue.

MAIN RISK

One substantial risk is to believe that the product will sell on its own, and **underestimate the business development** endeavor; in other words, being so much hands on the project that the strategic alignment with the BU, and the business traction is missed by far.

Step 8: Entrepreneurial culture, company attractiveness, and societal impact

Intrapreneurship is not for elite: entrepreneurial mindset can blossom outside the intrapreneurs' incubation stricto sensu.

Intrapreneurship is a powerful lever to **reinforce the company attractiveness, transform the employee culture, and yield a societal impact**.

USE CASES

>> CORPORATE EMPLOYMENT BRANDING

How Google does it

⬎ Google Area 120 is a startup haven to prevent staff from leaving: this startup incubator lets some employees pursue their "20% projects" (those personal projects Google allows in a fifth of your working hours) full-time. Anyone wanting to sign up would submit a business plan and, if accepted, spend several months working solely on that idea.

⅃ In Germany, a series of large companies are creating Corporate Startups programs to **attract young graduates** with a startup culture, and way of working.

>> SPREADING ENTREPRENEURIAL SKILLS

How Orange does it

The involvement of HR is paramount in intrapreneurship, not only in contributing to make the intrapreneurial incubation a safe and rewarding experience for the employee, but also in embracing the big picture of how intrapreneurship can **enrich the company culture**.

⅃ Orange has identified 6 skills that an employee should acquire: listening / responding / customer empathy, impactful communication, collaborative working, entrepreneurial spirit, and hard skills related to data and software fields. The **training for entrepreneurial spirit** starts with the ability to **Dare** and Take Initiatives, and a first e-learning module: Become a Player of your Future.

Intrapreneurs act as agents of change: other collaborators are impacted when they see their colleague pitching, when they contribute to an intrapreneur project, or when they adopt intrapreneur way of completing an innovation project, a mix of determination, listening, and frugality. Corresponding events and online communications demystify entrepreneurial spirit, and make it viral.

For the most mature companies, entrepreneurial skills are embedded into talent management, managerial posture, objectives, mobility and career evolution, and a comprehensive managers training toward intrapreneurship is rolled-out.

>> SOCIETAL IMPACT

How Red Cross, BNP Paribas, LVMH, SNCF, Airbus do it

Citizens feel more and more concerned by our societal environment, ranging from climate change to sustainable development: they want to act for good. No surprise that this translates within the companies they work for. Concurrently, CEOs realize that CSR is not only for communication, but that their companies have to be part of the planet solutions. 'Good washing' tends to disappear, and leaves space to a true connection between business and acting for good, accommodating positive social and environmental impact with immediate profitability.

Some companies support their employees in engaging in societal actions, and B Corp Label highlights these companies who make a positive impact on society.

↘ Microdon offers employees to subtract a few euros from their salary to the benefit of solidarity actions. Microdon addresses 250,000 employees from various companies. It also runs with Casino (food distribution) consumers, arising to 1 M€ collect from the set-up of the system.

Likewise, many programs for intrapreneurs have included a focus on **societal impact criteria in the call for projects**:

⊾ Red Cross opens its intrapreneurship program (12 days coaching over 6 months, 30% released time) to employees, volunteers, and students from institutes specialized in sanitary and social training: it looks for projects with a strong potential of social impact;

⊾ Intra4Good initiated by BNP Paribas is a community which connects intrapreneurs who pursue a project with a social impact. BNP Paribas, Danone and Engie have also partnered to launch a wonderful joint intrapreneurship program #Intrapreneurs4Good. The evening of intrapreneurs' pitchs in December 2019 brought together the three CEOs Isabelle Kocher, Emmanuel Faber and Jean-Laurent Bonnafé, who provided their support. It converges with BNP Paribas intrapreneur program, People'sLab4Good: in 2 seasons, 27 intrapreneurs were supported through 20 days training over 4 months – 25% free time per employee, and 7 countries, and 23 entities were involved; it is supported by CSR department, and aims at transforming ideas seeds in viable projects, conciliating employees' activity with benefits for society;

⊾ LVMH program for intrapreneurs DARE (Disrupt, Act, and Risk to be an Entrepreneur) welcomes projects covering the future of luxury to environment and gender parity;

↘ SNCF (the stations activity part) has launched its 2018 season with a prism on sustainable innovation: one of the projects, urbans asset for territories, examines how abandoned stations can find a second life;

↘ Airbus BizLab at Madrid introduces intrapreneurship as a combination of innovation, personal development, and societal impact.

↘ The book 'Transform your company from the inside: the social intrapreneur guide', by Emmanuel de Lutzel will take you through 20 stories of social intrapreneurs.

KEY QUESTIONS

Take into account entrepreneurial culture, company attractiveness, and societal impact through these questions:

- Can intrapreneurship improve the attractiveness of your company for future employees?

- How to communicate about the program externally to the different targets? Probably students won't see the same benefits in intrapreneurship as experienced candidates;
- How to spread entrepreneurial culture beyond the selected intrapreneurs, and use intrapreneurs as agents of change?
- Will you marry intrapreneurship with the CSR action?

MAIN RISK

One substantial risk is to **confine intrapreneurship approach to innovation, and new business**, stifling intrapeneurship to connect with a broader employee experience, and culture, including the wish to act for good.

Step 9: Innovation ecosystem

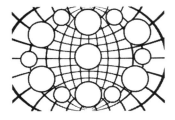 Intrapreneurship is part of a **broader innovation ecosystem** that includes new business models, digital acceleration, open innovation, and cultural transformation. The challenge is to figure out the right interweaving of innovation programs.

USES CASES

>> INNOVATION LABS TYPOLOGY

Innovation labs are soaring: in extension of traditional R&D, their purpose is yet different. We highlight 4 archetypes in this ecosystem:

- One archetype is based on former work I conducted in the course of a professional thesis at HEC Business School: it's the rapid innovation lab.
- The ultimate typology is the outcome of a joint work with Pierre Foullon, an enlightened student at Telecom ParisTech Master IREN. It capitalizes on Sihem Jouini analysis of 2012: Sihem is Associate Professor at HEC Business School, and outstanding

Director 2 streams (Majeures): Innovation & Entrepreneurship, and Innovation & Design.

- The 4 types of innovation labs which pan out are:
  - o **Disruptive labs for new business models;**
  - o **Rapid innovation labs: agile and speedy execution;**
  - o **Open innovation lab, aiming at cooperation;**
  - o **Innovation culture lab, propagating a audacity, and initiative spirit.**

>> DISRUPTIVE LABS

How Axa, Pernod-Ricard, Google, Air Liquide, Danone do it

Disruption combines a breakthrough business model with a gap in knowledge: through **revisited value proposition**, and original "value network" as says Clayton Christensen, it induces a reshuffling in consumption habits. A disruptive lab aims at snorting disruption, and bringing its company ahead of it, or by anticipating disruptors' threats as well. Disruptive innovation centers are therefore present in companies whose priority is to **renew their markets, and position themselves as leaders with creative business models**.

⬎ Kamet is AXA **startups studio** dedicated to the creation of disruptive insurance companies. Its objective is "to imagine, initiate, launch, and escort several disruptive InsurTech projects". Stéphane Guinet, Kamet's founder, presents Kamet as a startup that builds startups. Kamet has designed **a**

93

specific process to develop new business models: every 6 months, it unearths 40 ideas for new businesses, selects 8 of them, and staffs creative projects with seasoned entrepreneurs; following preliminary prototypes, 4 ventures are selected to be incubated over 1 year; they benefit from the agility of the studio, while having at their disposal AXA's know-how and expertise throughout the world;

↘ In France, agencies like Kador, 321founded, Mach49 'Disrupting InsideOut', Barefoot & Co, Mantu, La Piscine, Possible Future, RedStart, Founders Future, Alacrité France (Alacrity Global / Wesley Clover), ou Anova by Quantmetry, have shaped more or less **startups studio services for corporates**: they brainstorm with corporates about new business ideas, connect best ideas with boldest entrepreneurs, staff the venture team, and build solutions at a fast pace; sometimes they act on behalf of the corporation, or take shares in the venture. Five by Five looks for new business models with a distinctive value proposition: they help corporates **transform their unexplored potential and underutilized assets** (such as datasets, knowhow, infrastructures, talents) into new business opportunities;

↘ Breakthrough Innovation Group (BIG) of Pernod Ricard is a team of 10 people headed by Alain Dufossé, BIG's Managing Founder and Director. The objective is to **shake up usage by developing new products and services that will radically change and improve the consumer experience**: BIG works at inventing conviviality's future, adopting Blue Ocean strategy, capturing new demand in an uncontested corporate space;

⅂ Google X (or X), **the "Moonshot Factory"**, is a center of breakthrough innovation, and more specifically breakthrough technologies. "Projects target huge problems, and invent and launch "moonshot" technologies with a view to make the world a radically better place." explains Astro Teller, founder of Google X. X is a team of inventors and entrepreneurs from a wide variety of backgrounds. One of their noteworthy principles is to run as fast as they can at all the hardest parts of a problem, and **try to prove that something can't be done**: X actively embraces failure. Among the projects graduated, we find the Self-Driving Car (Waymo), Smart Contact Lens, Loon project, Google Glass, Google Wing allowing delivery by drone;

⅂ Air Liquide I-Lab founder, Gregory Olocco, explains how i-Lab, Air Liquide's open innovation laboratory, "combines a Think-Tank with a Corporate Garage approach" (confer Steve Jobs) and **intrapreneur mindset.** It has two main missions:

- Identifying **disruptive innovations**, representing threats or opportunities on core business, that challenge the 'operational excellence' mold; and then, refining market positioning, discussing strategic scenarios with business units;
- Detecting **opportunities for new business**, outside of mainstream activities, 'the third horizon of

innovation', involving completely new product/service and/or revisited business model.

⮷ Danone Innovation Accelerator General Manager, Manuela Borella, is leading one of the first successful multinational incubators: it combines **startups studio and digital acceleration,** acting as project entrepreneur on behalf of local structures. The objective is to bring growth and new capabilities to the company. The Danone Innovation Accelerator is all about **consumer intimacy**, and comprehension of unsolved pain points.

>> RAPID INNOVATION LABS

How Lockheed, O2, Airbus, Seb, Thales do it

These innovation centers, or digital factories, focus on speed. Speed can bring an unfair advantage, the ability to outsmart competition by reacting quickly, or to enter new markets, and become a threat to incumbents. Speed helps to focus on the most impactful features: "**the faster, the better**" as they say at Google.

⮷ Lockheed Skunk Works first team leader, Kelly Johnson, claims: "We are defined not by the technologies we create but by the process in which we create them." Skunk Works is the Advanced Development Program (ADP) division of Lockheed Martin. This internal organization aimed at stimulating the group's innovation, and developing new technologies, particularly in the aerospace sector. Probably one of the oldest "Lab" (founded in 1943), the group remained famous for its capacity to innovate. Lockheed Martin Skunk Works secret formula was the **rapid development of disruptive solutions through high autonomy, and modular operations**;

ↄ O2 Enterprise Lab division is driven by strong values of speed and quality explains Shomila Malik, former Lab Director. Players in the mobile industry are constantly seeking innovation, and are capable of inventing new solutions quickly. Agility has become the watchword of this innovation center. The main objective here is the development of **beta products to penetrate the market quickly**. Autonomy is an overarching enabler, and management remains very light: operations are similar to those of a startup. Ideas are prototyped quickly (a few days) after presentation and selection by the management team. Openness is another essential principle of O2 Enterprise Lab: open at the front end and in execution, open apis, open source, beta testing. Openness is also necessary as O2 Lab lets others bring the product through industrialization: getting 'buy in' is not a push but a pull: creating desire first;

ↄ Airbus Protospace follows the threat of uberisation of the sector (SpaceX). Protospace is a corporate FabLab. It provides each employee with the necessary tools, collocating design and prototyping skills, and to create on the Skunk model, materializing quickly emerging concepts. **Speed is at the**

heart of the complex, claims Vincent Loubière, Lead Technologist in the Emerging Technologies and Concepts team at Airbus, Founder and Leader of Airbus Protospace. Operating on an agile model, the team encourages creating and iterating according to its motto "Lead by Demonstration". Management is close to "startup" model, and openness is welcome through startups, universities or large companies who can bring together diverse skills;

↘ Seb corporate FabLab, and Thales Digital Factory rank also in this category of innovation lab oriented toward acceleration.

↘ The Rapid Innovation Model we designed at HEC Business School aggregates 4 fundamental principles:

1. **Autonomy**, the engine of creativity and speed;
2. **Creative tension** or the art of translating ideas into elegant experimentation, adopting a collective and iterative 'test and learn' framework; time-boxed projects put a positive tension on the team;
3. **Strategic alignmen**t: alignment with the core, creating a desire for change, unfolding opportunities deriving from the innovations developed, involving a shared innovation portfolio, and nurturing a network of innovation peers and relationships, to facilitate innovation acceptance;
4. **Modular design** allows innovation to be split into modules. In the same way as APIs in IT, this design

makes it possible for others to create value on top of your platform, and to retain an innovation capital potentially reused on several projects.

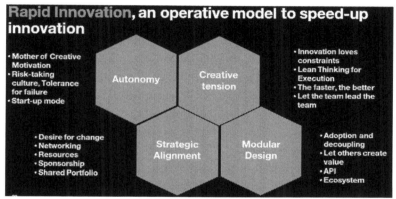

(source: https://buff.ly/2GZvqAa)

>> OPEN INNOVATION AND CO-CREATION LABS

How Airbus, Unibail, Orange, Crédit Agricole, BNP Paribas do it

These labs have a focus on **collaboration with startups**, partners or users, involving information sharing, and co-design to innovate. This model is more commonly referred to as Open Innovation.

Open innovation can happen at the front-end of the innovation process, during the ideation phase, later on, during the development process, by combining technologies, API modules, and know-how, or at the end, during the commercialization process, by sharing customer base, and distribution channels.

⟍ Airbus BizLab is an aerospace incubator based on an open innovation model combining both startups, and Airbus intrapreneur skills. It was founded by Bruno Guttieres, who is now Head of Mobility Orchestration & Collaborative Innovation at Alstom. The incubation program takes place over 6 months, allowing startups to share their knowledge with experts from the group in various fields. The most innovative projects are selected and financed by the firm. By **welcoming intrapreneurs' projects as well as startups**, Airbus stimulates internal innovation concurrently to opening the innovation engine to other ecosystems, and moving beyond the 'Not Invented Here' syndrome;

⟍ The Mixer is a startup accelerator belonging to the Unibail group, the largest commercial real estate company in Europe. It offers a support for 16 weeks whose main objective is to accelerate business between startups and Unibail. After a selection period, entrants have access to the teams, infrastructures and commercial portfolios of the real estate group. The program is organized with 6 main themes (**co-development** with Unibail, coaching and mentoring, funding strategies, prototyping, hosting of startups and events) to foster future commercial partnerships;

⟍ Orange Fab network of accelerators follows a similar objective: it covers 14 locations, and offers a 3-months accelerator program, searching for startups with existing products, looking for **growth and distribution** opportunities, mainly in the telecom and digital industries;

⊿ The Village by CA Paris is the open-innovation incubator set by Crédit Agricole bank and headed by Fabrice Marsella. It looks at detecting and supporting the **next French unicorns in FinTech**, and other industries. It **brings startups closer to large companies** (Sanofi, PSA, Sodexo, Avril, BETC...), which want to transform their models.

⊿ BNP Paribas bank operates startups accelerator programs called BNP Fintech, and BNP Innov and Connect, in a dedicated open innovation space WAI.

>> INNOVATION CULTURE AND INTRAPRENEURSHIP LABS

How Michelin, Safran do it

To **spread a culture of innovation** within corporations, many tools involve participatory innovation, crowdsourcing of ideas through challenges, and enticing intrapreneurship and entrepreneur spirit among employees. Thus, corporations mobilize collective intelligence as well as they recognize employees contribution, and increase their engagement.

⊿ Michelin, market leader in tires, has been under increasing competitive pressure from globalization in recent years. To keep pace, Michelin's innovation center has set up various tools to help spread a culture of innovation, such as

InnovaGo, Innov'up **challenges**, Bibspace social network or the Michelin Incubator Program Office;

⌲ Safran **FabLab** intended to breathe a culture of service, digital, innovation, and agility in a hardware manufacturing environment, and **welcomes every employee's ideas**. Ideas with high potential were supported into business through all stages including prototyping. Managers were part of the ecosystem: the idea had to get their buy-in just like from any other partner of the ecosystem.

Obviously all programs for intrapreneurs described previously belong to this Culture and Intrapreneurship Lab archetype.

Quite naturally **intrapreneurship blends with open innovation** with startups: "intrapreneurs can be considered as best open innovation project managers" states Raphaël Thobie, co-founder of CreateRocks innovation agency. Startups can boost the intrapreneurial spirit by mixing squads. The **Intrapreneurs Marketplace** paves the way for multi-corporations co-innovation projects. Some programs welcome business units' projects, merging intrapreneurship with rapid innovation lab. The matrix below summarizes the typology.

Disruptive

Tools/Approaches: Business Model Canvas, Disruptive innovation, Blue Ocean

Open Innovation

Tools/Approaches: Open Innovation, Design Thinking

Culture of Innovation & intrapreneurship

Tools/Approaches: Business Model Canvas, Design Thinking, Lean Start-up, Scaling-up

Rapid Innovation

Tools/Approaches: Agile, Scrum, Lean Startup

(Source: https://buff.ly/2klz0WK)

>> BOARD OF INNOVATION MATRIX

Board of Innovation agency has drafted an innovation matrix, to shape different devices "to discover patterns, develop focused capabilities, and **prioritize efforts based on the innovation maturity of the organization**".

Among the 4 archetypes and 16 actions below, intrapreneurship belongs to the right part 'Internal focus', from sparking interest 'Low investment - Experimenter' to transforming the organization 'High investment - Builder'.

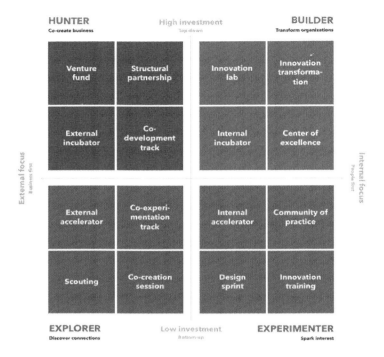

KEY QUESTIONS

Answering these questions helps to align intrapreneurship with the innovation ecosystem:

- What innovation initiatives have been recently developed from search for new business models, digital acceleration, to open innovation, and cultural transformation?
- How can intrapreneurship reinforce them, and create untapped opportunities?

- On which new aspect should focus the program for intrapreneurs in complement to the existing devices: soaring ideas, idea transformation into business, employees' engagement, societal impact?
- Which synergies should be developed?

MAIN RISK

One substantial risk is to **set the program for intrapreneurs aside**, and let it run as a black-box, whereas it interweaves naturally with innovation ecosystem, and should be transversal to business.

Step 10: Value creation, key metrics, and intrapreneurship business canvas

CHALLENGE

Ultimately the **value created** by intrapreneurship will be questioned. It is far from an all-or-nothing game, solely deriving from the success of the project.

Business value (revenues, branding, competitive bundling) doesn't need to overshadow employees assets (personal development, cultural transformation, company attractiveness), and societal impact (social, environmental impacts). Good to know: it's better to define your success **metrics** before the start than at the end!

USES CASES

With a group of organizations engaged in intrapreneurship (Air France, GRDF, Orange, Safran, Professor Véronique Bouchard - emlyon business school) facilitated by Sophie Ravel from the Ministry of Economy (Bercy Open Lab), with Yasmine Le Guyader, State Brand platform strategist, we have designed an **Intrapreneurship Label** for corporations and organizations. It includes a list of KPIs.

Extending this work, I have sorted out 3 types of metrics:

>> BUSINESS METRICS

- **Engagement**: number of applications, proving program appeal, and creating an innovative ideas capital including ideas not selected;
- **Footprint**: number of countries involved; progression of intrapreneurs projects sponsored by business units, evolution of business units acceptance for intrapreneurs projects; number of business units committed to the intrapreneurship approach, or with a budding program for intrapreneurs;
- **Speed** of transformation into business, proving process agility during incubation phase, and landing / scale-up phase: time to market of intrapreneurs innovations;
- **Quality, and beat of customer insights**: research (interviews), and experiments (MVP testing) of intrapreneurs projects; connection of intrapreneurs projects with customers' expectations / pain points; connection with corporate strategy;
- **Business transformation**: number / % of intrapreneurs projects transitioned into business, internally, and externally; new line of business opened, and corresponding revenues; bundling with existing offer, bringing 'unfair advantage' for customers or vs competition; communication

opportunity for business units, proof of innovation capability; quick wins completed;

- **ROI and learning curve** of program for intrapreneurs.

>> TRANSFORMATION / HR METRICS

- **Engagement**: number and diversity of applicants, and intrapreneurs selected; number of training hours delivered; level of engagement of intrapreneurs (agents of change) vs average engagement level of employees; number of employees impacted (each intrapreneur might be contaminating 300 to 500 other employees within the company; another indicator is the pool of contributors to strengthen the intrapreneur project); internal communication articles about intrapreneurship; indication of entrepreneurship culture spreading; evolution of employees perception of their company (innovative, open, ...); evolution of company attractiveness linked to intrapreneurship, great place to work at;

- **Return of experience**: quality of intrapreneurship experience, and intrapreneurs satisfaction rate; satisfaction rate of managers involved in intrapreneurship: BUs managers, and managers ceding resources;

- **Professional posture**: evolution of senior managers participating in the Jury selection, acting as budding VCs (Venture Capitalists) with startups; feedback shared at the intrapreneurs certification jury, and number of intrapreneurs certified; visibility of intrapreneurs; inclusion of intrapreneurship in company's values, and management system: taking into account facilitation of intrapreneurship in managers' role and objectives, entrepreneurial spirit in employees skills and roles definition, in leadership profile or talent management.

>> SOCIETAL IMPACT METRICS

One can measure its contribution to UN sustainable development goals, and through the B Corp label. The B Corp impact assessment examines how your company is better for your workers, community, customers, and the environment, and presents several societal impact domains:

- **Diversity, civic engagement & giving**, addressing underserved populations;
- **Environmental** products & services, environmental practices, land / office / plant, energy / water / materials, emissions / water / waste, suppliers & transportation.

>> INNOVATION METRICS

⌙ Tristan Kromer, Innovation Ecosystems & Startups Consultant, describes how to build metrics for an innovation program:

- It's always a good idea to agree on the metrics for success before getting started, and to **make the objectives clear before setting metrics**: "Go Innovate" is not a strategy, and it's not an objective;
- ROI is a lagging indicator that takes a while to show up; don't be afraid to use **vanity metrics** like "We generated 746 new ideas!"; but vanity metrics bite back: of those 746 ideas, only 20 were chosen for acceleration, and 10 were killed soon after; ultimately 2 ideas were chosen as "winners," but neither was accepted into the main business unit, so they just ended up sitting in limbo! Since no ideas from the first year were seen to fruition, only 98 ideas are submitted in the second year showing a decreasing metric...
- **Choose metrics that are leading indicators of the change targeted**, and look for things to measure that will ultimately contribute to ROI: teams with more insights about the market have a better chance of success; to get more insights about the market, teams need to run experiments and research; therefore, the more research and experiments, the better the odds of success: start measuring whether the teams are running experiments (**experiment velocity**) or generating insights (**insight velocity**) each week;

- Showing an innovation project will be unsuccessful generates an immediate ROI simply by shutting it down; **saving $1 million by shutting down a bad project** isn't as sexy as earning $1 million in new revenue, but it's just as valid (metric = cost per insight or cost per iteration);
- **Go talk to your C-level customer,** and reach an agreement on what metrics to measure before we get started.

>> INTRAPRENEURSHIP SOCIAL BUSINESS MODEL CANVAS

Intrapreneurs projects are trained to sum-up their solution in a business model canvas: it works for the program for intrapreneurs as well!

Fulfilling the 10 steps of this guide directly leads you to complete your intrapreneurship canvas. This enables you to **check the consistency** of the various squares, and their relationship, in the systematic approach which characterizes the business model canvas.

1. Step 1 "Reason Why, and strategic alignment" fits in Value Proposition square, like step 2 "Value Proposition", which also addresses Customer Segment;
2. Step 3 "Sponsorship" goes in Key Partners so as step 6 "Business units Commitment";

3. Step 4 "Intrapreneurship process" and step 7 "Exit scenarios, biz dev, and scale-up" feed Key Activities, and Channels;
4. Step 6 "Intrapreneurs coaching, and resources" feeds Key resources, and Customer Relationships;
5. Step 9 "Innovation ecosystem' belongs to Key Partners square;
6. Step 8 "Entrepreneurial culture, company attractiveness, and societal impact" and step 10 "Value creation, and metrics" feed Cost/Revenue squares as well as Social/Environmental.

Intrapreneurship Business Model Canvas

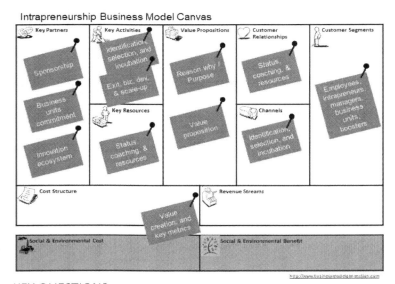

KEY QUESTIONS

This series of questions helps you to define the best metrics:

- What metrics will be appropriate to monitor the achievement of the purpose defined in step 1? How do they show how the initial problem is solved: bringing new products and services to market more quickly, retaining your best staff, and attracting the best candidates, adopting more agile and customer-oriented ways of innovating, creating an environment where employees take initiatives, making a societal impact, in consistency with CSR engagement?
- Are these metrics easy to calculate? What are the sources of data? Which frequency is relevant?
- Do you have metrics for the different stages of the program?
- Do your metrics need to evolve according to program maturity? Expectations might vary from the first season to the nth season.

MAIN RISK

One substantial risk is to define **metrics that don't fit with innovation and company transformation**, and stick only to the traditional business, and common indicators.

+20 intrapreneurs exemplary stories

APPROACH

We collected the following success stories in autumn 2019, by asking intrapreneurship managers to spot their innovation champions, and forward them the following questions:

1. What is the business of your corporate startup? Did the intrapreneur project transition to a corporate business line, or to a spin-out startup?
2. How did the program for intrapreneurs help you? At the project level, and the personal development level?
3. Why this business could not have been developed through the traditional system?
4. What are the key figures that you would like to share about your business?
5. What learnings would you like to share with fledgling intrapreneurs?

A story is not only a success if the intrapreneur project hit the market; the learning experience for the intrapreneur is equally meaningful, even though his project may have been stopped.

Experiences collected are incredibly diverse: they embark **seasoned to recently hired employees**, **single intrapreneur or pairs**. They **exit** in new product or business line, internal process for transformation, exploration of digital new landscape, new business unit, subsidiary or startups, most often funded by the corporation.

Intrapreneures' projects counterbalance those of of intrapreneurs, and this gender equity is good news for innovation!

They all have in common one powerful trigger: the **passion of savvy intrapreneurs that drives them to exceed obstacles, bounce, persist, and drag others along**!

They demonstrate how the experience has been intense, and how they and the company have collected **priceless learnings**, beyond the necessary business metric, displaying new outlooks for engagement, and initiatives.

Airbus: Alberto Toledo Garrote, air traffic demand

Alberto Toledo Garrote is Airline Scientist - Network Planning (Commercial) at Airbus in Spain. He joined 9 years ago. Alberto highlights how intrapreneurship has **focused him on customers and market understanding for his digital service.**

What is the business of your corporate startup? Did the intrapreneur project transition to a corporate business line, or a spin-out startup?

Our project consists on designing a new **machine learning platform to foresee the passenger flow** travelling for a specific route.

When we met Bertrand, HO Airline Science (part of the Airbus Digital Transformation Office) he proposed us to **integrate the Airbus project in Airline Science platform**. Now we are part of this great team.

The Airbus BizLab provided to us all the resources that we needed for the project development, including the company network, methods and tools. It is a very amazing experience for any employee that I really recommend. Now, I am very happy, and proud to see how we do our bit for the company strategy.

How did the program for intrapreneurs help you? At the project level, and the personal development level?

The program was definitely one of the pillars to ensure the success of the project. BizLab is a really **business oriented** accelerator, and it is really cool, because no matter how good your idea is if you don't know how to meet the market expectations.

We learnt a lot about how to **understand the market expectations** and then how to communicate and sell your ideas, catching the interest of your customers.

It was really important to follow the acceleration roadmap to see real results in a short period of time.

Why this business could not have been developed through the traditional system?

Probably, because the main interlocutors needed for developing the project are really big companies that are not easily to reach if you don't have the support of a big brand like Airbus. Having **Airbus as a sponsor** means a lot in terms of confidence, and representation.

What are the key figures that you would like to share about your business?

I think that we have a good example with our project to understand why the digitalization is so important for the industry in general and particularly for the aviation.

Due to the market uncertainty, the financial risk that an airline might assume when a new route is opened use to be around 10 million dollars. Investing only a few of thousands to simulate the actual possible scenarios through the artificial intelligence, you can minimize this risk a lot, having a margin of confidence higher than 92%, that is very good in comparison with the state of the art.

For the air transport industry it means a **more efficient and greener business**.

What learnings would you like to share with fledgling intrapreneurs?

Putting passion and work are necessary conditions but not sufficient. You need to believe in your project and **trust in your coach** if you want to see your ideas take off.

Air France: Benjamin Lalanne, Smooss

Benjamin Lalanne is Senior Manager, Network Planning and Revenue Management at Air France, which he joined 6 years ago. Since June 2018, he's Cofounder and CEO of a fresh startup resulting from intrapreneurship. Benjamin explains how intrapreneurship is **a perfect sandbox for new business, combining agility with access to customers, and data.**

What is the business of your corporate startup? Did the intrapreneur project transition to a corporate business line, or a spin-out startup?

Smooss is a b2b startup developing SaaS solution (in the cloud) for travel and events industry partners.

We are working around the concept of **post-booking optimization** to improve our partners' revenue, decrease their disruption costs, and improve their customers' experience. Travels are subject to changes, and for instance, business travelers might desperately want to get a seat on a full plane. Benjamin's service identifies flexible customers, open to taking another plane, and free their seat, with an extra-bonus, and makes the swing easy, and smooth.

After less than 1 year of incubation, a **spin-out startup** has been created. Air France participates in funding, and takes shares.

How did the program for intrapreneurs help you? At the project level, and the personal development level?

Program for intrapreneurs is clearly **the perfect sand box** to launch new ideas. It offers **trainings** to learn design thinking, agile state of mind, and moreover you have indeed a **direct link with your customers**, and the know-how of **corporate knowledge** to test and adapt your concept.

For a B2B startup, it is a unique and perfect setup. By experience we know that with airlines it is very difficult to get **access to data** if you are from the external world.

First the team has worked on personal time, then **time allocation** was granted by the jury: an equivalent of one person full time when aggregating partial time of 3 people, over one year.

Why this business could not have been developed through the traditional system?

Innovation is part of Air France DNA, but by definition with innovation inherent business case is always difficult to assess. Therefore new ideas which need to have their business hypothesis to be validated are confronted to other recurring corporate projects, more secure, during the prioritization process.

Even with promising business cases and frugal mode, our project could not have been launched before 2 years because of the **backlog**.

Moreover our innovative project implied use of new technology, and impact on Air France internal IT system. To be compliant with Air France IT security chart, we would also have delayed the development process of our solution, and our MVP would have not been frugal anymore!

What are the key figures that you would like to share about your business?

- Post-booking market represents a potential of €100b in airline industry only;
- **1 M€ additional revenue for Air France** thanks to our first product, in 6 months.

What learnings would you like to share with fledgling intrapreneurs?

Firstly, intrapreneurship can be the perfect setup, as you can test your ideas and business hypothesis, with the customers of your business. Moreover within your company you will benefit from an incredible knowledge (product, legal, social, communication, finance…) accessible to you as long as you do not forget to **involve every stakeholder from the beginning**.

Secondly, you will have to find the right balance between startups disruptive methods and corporate processes. Startups methods are not 100% adapted to corporate world but corporate process can rapidly kill innovation. Once again you will need to involve as earliest as possible your stakeholders and especially your Top Level management to get a wild (blue) card.

Air Liquide: Renaud Thiard, purified air in buildings (UMPAI)

Renaud Thiard is intrapreneur at Air Liquide Open Innovation Lab. He's working on Air Quality business development. Previously, he was Innovation Manager in the Engineering Division for 3 years, and Industrial Risk Management for 4 years. Renaud feels that intrapreneurship provides **precious visibility to convince sponsors, and a dizzying skills set**.

What is the business of your corporate startup? Did the intrapreneur project transition to a corporate business line, or a spin-out startup?

The business consists in leveraging Air Liquide gas cleaning know-how to **provide purified air in buildings** and bring additional measurable health, comfort & energy saving to the commercial real estate industry.

After several months of internal research, lobbying and scenario analysis with my partner, we identified and convinced **two strong sponsors**. They helped us transfer the project into the corporate **business line dedicated to new markets & technologies.**

How did the program for intrapreneurs help you? At the project level, and the personal development level?

Thanks to the program, I had the "uncommon" opportunity to dedicate **full time** to the project. I got also trained to most tools and methodologies to accelerate **innovation**, had access to a **network** of entrepreneurs & mentors who really helped me iterate and challenge myself. (especially through the partnership with Techstars, during 1,5 months). As this program was quite visible, it gave me the chance to be **exposed,** and convince directly my company's highest executives.

Regarding personal development, and whatever final "exit" of the project, this 3 year polyvalent experience provided **as many skills as one can gets in 9 years**. I consider it as a personal accelerator which reinforced my self-confidence and self-awareness

Why this business could not have been developed through the traditional system?

As this business was **too far from my company's native markets** and too disruptive in terms of innovation, it would have been virtually impossible to develop and incubate it into the traditional system.

Core Business P&L profitability requirements are in fact incompatible with risk associated with opening new markets. This was precisely the reason why the Open Innovation Lab, was created at Air Liquide: create ambitious "blue ocean" but legitimate opportunities.

What are the key figures that you would like to share about your business?

In 3 years of development:

- More than 100 customers interviewed, 20 commercial leads, **4 signed contracts, 1 full demonstrator;**
- 2 Air Liquide people working full time, over 25 contributing Air Liquide people, 8 internal sponsors;
- **1 million € internal funding** obtained to accelerate the project into a corporate business line.

What learnings would you like to share with fledgling intrapreneurs?

- **Start from the pain** rather than the solution;
- **Think big and test small;**
- Be comfortable in dealing with **corporate ambiguity;**
- Keep a **high speed pace,** and at the same time **be patient** & resilient.

BNPP: Bruno Nicole et Aurélie Vallée, Neymo (ney-mo.com)

Bruno Nicole is Neymo Chief Marketing Officer at BNP Paribas Personal Finance, where he has worked for 8 years, and Aurélie Vallée is Neymo Operations Manager. They co-founded Neymo in 2018. They share how intrapreneurship triggered them to **take risks, for a "roller coaster" experience, aside from the traditional career path, and attract much expertise** on their project.

What is the business of your corporate startup? Did the intrapreneur project transition to a corporate business line, or a spin-out startup?

Neymo is an intrapreneurship project born in BNP Paribas Personal Finance through a bottom-up internal challenge. We decided to develop and launch on the French market **a budget management mobile app for individuals** based on bank account data analysis.

This project is directly in line with BNP Paribas Personal Finance business, and based on opportunities created by a new regulation (PSD2) which came into effect in September.

It was a personal and professional challenge because when the project was selected, we had to choose between following our "classic" job or **jumping into a complete**

unknown adventure. Furthermore, it was the first intrapreneurship experience for BNP Paribas group.

After 9 months in a BNP Paribas incubator, we have created **a corporate business line** to continue the project. The project is reporting to an internal board of Exco members.

How did the program for intrapreneurs help you? At the project level, and the personal development level?

The BNP Paribas Personal Finance program for intrapreneurs called **Bivwak** was a really incredible initiative, and we were excited to join in.

We were lucky to have multiple **internal and external experts** around the project even if we quickly felt that having too much kindness and people around us could be a little anxious. We thought we were a little team of 3 people with 3 external technical consultants but most of the time we were more than that in the room.

We have been **fully dedicated** to the development of the project during the incubation period which lasted **9 months** at the heart of Paris. We had to avoid making too much reporting but also to find the right experts at the right time and it was the most difficult part.

At the end of the day, the incubation phase was really successful as we were able to continue the adventure within BNPP group.

From a personal perspective, it was really challenging to literally **"live" for the project** during 9 months without knowing if it would be possible to go further; even though starting from nothing, we were proud of our "MVP"!

Those 9 months have really been a human experience, and we were not prepared to live such **"roller coaster" experience**. Every time we think we've reached the finish line, we were starting a new race.

Why this business could not have been developed through the traditional system?

In the traditional system, it would have been nearly impossible to have something "live" in 9 months as it was mandatory to be very **agile** to do that.

- First of all, we got the possibility to develop our app on a **dedicated IT platform** with a dedicated IT support. It would have been impossible to develop such a project with internal IT systems;
- Secondly, during the intrapreneurship program, we had the opportunity to **dare without being afraid to fail**, and without compliance and legal constraints (for the MVP part). We needed a space free from Group processes in order to launch the MVP, and prove the value before launching the Group validation process in terms of compliance and security;

- Thirdly, we have been **100% dedicated** to the project with a deadline to prove the value;
- Fourthly, we got the support of the **General Management** that helped us a lot to launch the project;
- Finally, as we often said, it was really engaging to have **people involved in their own project,** and benefiting from the support of a large company. We often thought that the goal was too difficult to reach, but we know now that it is possible when you are motivated.

What are the key figures that you would like to share about your business?

We met 200 testers since the beginning of the project, and our app has just been launched on the market, but we hope to reach **1000 users of our first beta version** by the end of the year.

What learnings would you like to share with fledgling intrapreneurs? Is there a special strength in being 2?

- Benefit from a **strong sponsorship** at the right level is key for the project;
- Finding **allies**, and build a network of experts is important;
- You need **customer validation**, and regular feedback;
- Intrapreneurship is a question of **mindset**, human relationships and **team spirit;**
- **Idea is not everything; it's just a small ingredient.**

One of the great strengths of this adventure was to succeed in **building a team around two people** who were united as the core of the project. It was a precious support in this experience, particularly through the complementarity of skills, the ability to challenge ideas, or to take the necessary distance.

The binomial, once it works, it is utterly beneficial, and in our case it has been!

BNPP: Céline Pernot-Burlet (Agiles' Tribe & Happy Scribing)

Céline Pernot-Burlet joined BNPP 14 years ago, where she developed Graphic Facilitation. She is an alumni intrapreneur from 2015, creating not one but two projects: the Agiles' Tribe and Happyscribing. Céline is a vibrant example that intrapreneurship can give birth to **internal service lines, extending employees skills, and saving substantial costs.**

What is the business of your corporate startup? Did the intrapreneur project transition to a corporate business line, or a spin-out startup?

I've been leading 2 main intrapreneur projects at BNP Paribas for 4 years, the #tribudesagiles (Agiles' Tribe) and #happyscribing.

- The **#tribudesagiles** is a device that allows a collaborator who has a talent, a skill useful to the Group to carry out **short missions** in parallel with his daily activity. This is a new way of working that allows to diversify the missions of employees, and create commitment, as well as test, and disseminate new practices within the company: for instance, graphic facilitation, or facilitation of collective intelligence, storytelling, the art of the pitch, facilitation of round tables … Not only does the employee value new skills but it also reduces the costs of external services for the company;

- I created the #tribudesagiles to create **#happyscribing**. I was already passionate about graphic facilitation, and was looking for a way to popularize the practice internally. Graphic facilitation and sketchnote (method of taking notes) are tangible and playful tools that allow organizing your thoughts, to express your ideas, and to promote collaborative work. I am convinced that graphical facilitation is useful in all types of activity. Today I use it mainly to support projects with positive impacts.

The #tribudesagiles and #happyscribing are not intended to leave the group, they are completely integrated internally and transversely in the group, like **internal service lines**.

How did the program for intrapreneurs help you? At the project level, and the personal development level?

The program gave me **key tools** and knowledge of the **startup universe** (design thinking, pitch ...). Concretely, one of the modules that was most useful to me in the program is the audience mapping / sociogram.

At the beginning of my intrapreneurial experience, I was aiming at convince everyone (there are 180,000 employees at BNP Paribas ...). I was very disappointed when people I didn't know were spending more energy going against my project than helping me develop it!

Understanding the **motivations of people** (their "why"), the political games, the issues of each other, their priorities, allowed me to build a strategy to develop my project and register it in the long term:

1. **Do not try to convince people who will never be supportive** of your idea;
2. **Give priorities to the right actions**: try to convince the people who allow me to multiply my impact, convince people who can help me to convince other people ...

The program helped me on 2 soft skills:

1. Feel legitimate in the organization to **dare** to present my ideas / achievements / projects to top management;
2. Training and **coaching** allowed me to reinforce my self-confidence. I now dare to suggest things, I learned how to pitch, and even if the exercise is always stressful for me, I manage to speak in public more serenely than before.

Why this business could not have been developed through the traditional system?

The #tribudesagiles is a transversal project interesting in terms of economy, and HR. The idea was quite **disruptive**: it was assuming that the employee can leave his daily framework, and perform cross-functional missions without losing his position.

Developing such a project requires intrapreneur's tenacity and commitment. I had to prove by doing: completing 50 missions with a group of collaborators of my network, in parallel of my current activity, to nurture concrete proofs during my different pitches. This type of project must be embodied by collaborators who are **makers** ... It must show that it works concretely.

Same for #happyscribing. When I started performing graphic facilitation missions, many people saw it as a "wow effect", and did not perceive the real interest of the activity. It was truly a new way of working. **If innovation comes too early, it is likely not to be adopted.** So we had to do a lot of pedagogy, and show concretely, mission after mission, the usefulness of these new tools.

What are the key figures that you would like to share about your business?

In 4 years, the Agiles' Tribe has carried out 1400 missions, nearly 1,300 days representing more than **2 M€ of savings**.

Concurrently, 26 employees have joined the #happyscribing community, and completed **772 graphic facilitation missions**, representing 730 days of support. In 3 years, we have facilitated 87 introductory workshops on graphic facilitation, meaning over 1,500 trained employees.

This summer we co-organized the International Sketchnote Camp, the event that brings together the international community of sketchnoters every year: more than 170 sketchnoters took part in the event.

What learnings would you like to share with fledgling intrapreneurs?

Intrapreneurs have to be "makers", show that what you have in mind works. Mastering the art of pitch is essential to capture the attention of the people you want to convince, but **tangible proofs** of achievement, are also very important to develop your project, and stand overtime.

BNPP Luxembourg: Catherine Wurth, Finance4Good

Catherine Wurth joined BNPP 4 years ago to lead the CSR accelerator for innovation and socially responsible finance projects. She's likewise an intrapreneure, alumni 2018 of People'sLab4Good (BNPP program for intrapreneurs), and founder of Finance4Good at BNL (Luxembourg). Catherine shows how to **incorporate social into an innovative and business-driven service**, through intrapreneurship.

What is the business of your corporate startup? Did the intrapreneur project transition to a corporate business line, or a spin-out startup?

The idea of my intrapreneurial project is to launch a new savings product, Finance4Good. **Finance4Good** is a service that offers to **leverage one's savings to finance companies with social and environmental impact**, making use of the savings interests. A community to participate in events, and access to content on impact generated, is part of this device.

After the intrapreneurship program, the project has integrated the bank catalogue, and will be sold as **a new savings product** within BGL BNP Paribas.

How did the program for intrapreneurs help you? At the project level, and the personal development level?

The intrapreneurship program was first of all **training** on new working methods (design thinking, agile methods ...), public presentation, the world of startups, and social entrepreneurship.

It also allowed me to develop my project with **coaches**, and put in place a business plan and a strategy to convince investors in house.

The intrapreneurship program was a very **rich personal experience** that not only revealed my entrepreneurial spirit, but also created **strong links** with other people in my promo of People'sLab4Good as well as with the organizers.

Why this business could not have been developed through the traditional system?

This is a bank product for savings that would have been very difficult to launch without the structure of an existing bank behind. Yet the intrapreneurship program has boosted the implementation of Finance4Good for several reasons:

- An early-stage **bottom-up project** that would not have gone across the hierarchical ladders without having the visibility that the PL4G (People'sLab4Good) brought;
- A project of the **CSR** department far from the teams in charge of creating new products. PL4G allowed the project to set up a cross-functional team to design the new product;

- A lot of visibility also at the group level which allowed Finance4Good to have **high level sponsors** to allow prioritization compared to other projects.

What are the key figures that you would like to share about your business?

Hard to say since the product will only be officially launched in early 2020! Nevertheless the key motivation to launch this product was the fact that today **80% of millennials want to invest in a responsible way**. While the consumer can choose to buy organic and ethical, buy green energy, there is currently no product for responsible savings, which is accessible to all within BNP Paribas.

What learnings would you like to share with fledgling intrapreneurs?

It takes a lot of **energy** and **tenacity** to carry out a project. It is necessary to constantly **inspire, and motivate people around you** so that they operate the right levers. Being an intrapreneur is both enriching, and fulfilling. We are **active agents of change**.

Bouygues: Laurent Mareuge, Com'in

Laurent Mareuge began his career at Bouygues Travaux Publics in 2003 as a Methods and Works Manager, working on many major international tunnel, bridge, and civil engineering projects. He led the first Grand Paris Express civil engineering project in 2016, and became deputy project director in 2017. In 2019, he joined the Group's Intrapreneurship entity.

Laurent took the intrapreneurship opportunity to **bring digital tools, and artificial intelligence in the traditional business of construction**.

What is the business of your corporate startup? Did the intrapreneur project transition to a corporate business line, or a spin-out startup?

Com'in is a start-up created within Bouygues SA thanks to the intrapreneurship program "ICS" (Innovate as a Startup).

Com'in wants to **use the current capabilities of artificial intelligence to improve the environment of construction and industrial activities in urban areas**.

The first solution we are developing is an online disturbance monitoring and decision-making platform designed to reduce the negative impact of operations on the neighboring community.

This expert tool for decision support (choice to stop, modify or continue the work) allows answering on the action taken in coordination with all the members of the Com'in platform.

It can be to stop trucks engine running at 5:30 am, delay jackhammers work after 7am, ask collaborators to speak more quietly, use spray water against dust, ...

The aim is for the intrapreneur project to **transition to a corporate business line**.

How did the program for intrapreneurs help you? At the project level, and the personal development level?

The main advantages that I see in this framework are:

- **Coaching** with an accelerator that helps to structure the project quickly;
- Possibility to **work 100% on the project** from the acceleration phase;
- Quickly obtain the requested **funding** for the acceleration phase, which allows to organize to effectively confirm the Business Model and Business Plan;
- Benefit from the extremely wide **network** of the Group.

Why this business could not have been developed through the traditional system?

To give yourself every chance to launch a new activity, it is necessary to devote 100% of your time, and obtain the necessary funding to put the launch of the activity on the right track.

What are the key figures that you would like to share about your business?

- **5 construction/industrial sites equipped** with our solution in prototype phase within 6 months since the beginning of the acceleration phase;
- Winner of Bouygues Construction Innovation Competition 2018 - INNO CUP;
- Nominated for the Public Works Trophy 2019;
- Speaker at the Paris Symposium of MIT ILP: http://ilp.mit.edu/conference.jsp?confid=239&tabname=speakers;
- Speaker at the FRTP General Assembly of November 12, 2019.

What learnings would you like to share with fledgling intrapreneurs?

Do not hesitate to embark, because it is an extremely **exhilarating experience** even if it may stop at the end of the acceleration period.

And above all, **do not be discouraged** by the many obstacles that stand on the course!

Coca-Cola: Ioana Morogan, Les Assoiffés

Ioana Morogan is Associate Director New Business & Incubator teams at Coca-Cola European Partners, which she joined 10 years ago. She was caught by the intrapreneurial virus (66miles @Willa Paris Pionnières), and it has led her to create the corporate incubator Les Assoiffés (The Thirsty).

Ioana shares her tips to **build an intrapreneur path when there is no program for intrapreneurs in the corporation to show you the way.**

What is the business domain of your intrapreneur project? How did you evolve from an intrapreneur project to the Coca-Cola Incubation entity, les Assoiffés, which you manage currently?

I have **"self-proclaimed" myself as an intrapreneur** in 2017. I was working as a senior sales manager, and I had an idea of building a platform that connects our out-of-home customers, who have specific needs, to Food Tech start-up that have tailored solutions to those needs.

During 4 months, I have dedicated **one day a week** to implement the platform. I was helped by 66miles, an intrapreneur program powered by Willa, who helped me fast-track the solution.

In 2018, with a couple of fellows, I have built the **brand incubator**. We called it "Les Assoiffés". Thirsty of innovation, of new experiences, of learning with new eyes (that's our Manifesto). We have chosen the name Les Assoiffés because it describes our way of doing things. The evolution turned out to be a last-minute opportunity I have jumped in. A good interview with top management and some stars aligned. No secret recipe.

Our official mission is to create **a new business model that INCUBATE & GROW premium products on emerging categories** which require a different go-to-market model. Our untold mission (oups – it is not anymore!) is to shake up internal processes, contribute to more entrepreneurship mindset while we #WorkHardandPlayHarder (like really, it's in our DNA!).

How did you manage to get visibility to your project, time and resources? What skills did you particularly developed in this experience?

I had partners in crime from the beginning. Firstly, my line manager and N+2. They have just trusted me and gave me time.

Then, it is like an entrepreneur, you seek for money and support but with the ease of having everything on hand.

- I have built a draft business plan based on a vision & objectives & principles to achieve;

143

- I have identified who are my official and non-official sponsors, contributors, detractors;
- and look for a "company office" to raise funds.

Mad skills! I have developed **my punk side**. Like a rottweiler, I was defending my bone on a regular base. Defending the project in front of the rest of the organization, some trying to compare our KPI's with those applied to core business.

More classical, I have developed my **financial and supply chain** skills (hard!). We are a small team, in charge of the go-to-market process of a brand, including last-mile delivery topics.

You need to do everything with short budget (sounds weird for a big corporate!), and show quick wins. It helped you be **humble and creative while staying passionate**.

Why this business could not have been developed through the traditional system?

Innovation is about doing a lot of small things. It is also about **testing & learning**. Therefore, those "small things" have to be protected from core business. If they infuse into the traditional model, they will be, at best, deprioritized, or at worst, they will disrupt/ distract core system. The key question is how long you protect them? When do you scale?

What are the key figures that you would like to share about your business?

We have launched **4 new products on emerging categories in one year,** and collaborated with a portfolio of 700 customers in big cities like Paris and Bordeaux.

With the first incubated brand, **Appletiser**, we partnered with Too Good To Go to fight against day-to-day food waste (as the initial recipe of the product was made with waste/ unsold apples) + we are trying to optimize our supply chain with them.

We have launched our first **BtoB ecommerce platform with 100 customers** registered in less than one year. This was designed by a start-up we met at Station F on a Friday afternoon [Kol, a specialist in beverage delivery] ☺ Again, no theory, just constant open eyes.

What learnings would you like to share with fledgling intrapreneurs?

Long time I thought intrapreneur is a marketing-cool-etiquette. It is actually much more than that. It helps name what you are doing and it gives you access to a community and tailored tools. Mine are:

- Find your partner(s). **Don't be alone**;
- Find your **sponsors**. Make sure you have a mandate to do it. I relate a lot onto the pirate & corsair analogy. **Be a corsair,** otherwise you got killed at the

end. Corsairs were commissioned by a nation to fight with their own methods, they were legal;

- **Be prepared**. Exactly as an entrepreneur, you will need to build a business plan. Know your financial indicators. Show you can generate additional business and immaterial high value. Name it. Name the value you bring that can't fit into a P&L;
- Try to avoid normal project management process like 'steering committee". **Take your top management like your investment fund**. You need to align them on business indicators/ financial reviews and destination. See them on a quarterly basis, no more. It is too intrusive;
- **Map your organization**. Anticipate the scale phase, it can't be decided by others;
- **Know yourself.** Why are you doing this? Save the world, save your company, save yourself, break the rules, you don't know? Honestly, continue to ask yourself why you are doing it. It is your backbone when you will face ups and downs (yep, there will be some); and firstly because you will be passionate about what you are doing, and sometimes you have personal implication in it "you come up with the business case");
- Working for a big company is a unique **opportunity of scaling quickly**, have all Resources at hand. If you

succeed, the impact will be greater than if you would have launched your solution alone;

- Read **Business For Punks** by James Watt, the founder of BrewDog!

And **Enjoy**. Like really do. What an amazing opportunity you have to invent your own job and maybe the future of your company!

Engie: Sophie Guignard, Energy Bay

Sophie Guignard is Head of the Digital Platform Energy Bay, an intrapreneur project at Engie. Previously she spent 7 years at Engie as Digital Use Case Expert, Category Manager ICT & Digital, and 12 years at Thales at various management positions, notably at IT. Sophie proves that every **innovation starts by marking off the problem at stake**, and that you have to **dare to ask**, if you want help or agreement!

What is the business of your corporate startup? Did the intrapreneur project transition to a corporate business line, or a spin-out startup?

Energy Bay is a service **developed by Engie Digital, a corporate Business Line**. Energy Bay is a service acting as **a marketplace with the objective to reduce, and monetize overstocks in ENGIE assets**.

Energy Bay is offering an alternative to procurement teams that is this way able to source directly from a large catalog of products coming from multi-suppliers, and already stocked.

The value proposal is based on 3 pillars:

1. By connecting sellers to spare parts buyers, Energy Bay helps sellers monetize their overstocks;

2. By proposing a way to easily & quickly find the spare parts needed to maintain the assets, Energy Bay reduces unavailability;
3. And finally by giving a second life to the parts instead of remanufacturing new ones, **Energy Bay acts for the planet**, reducing CO_2 impact.

How did the program for intrapreneurs help you? At the project level, and the personal development level?

The intrapreneur program #66 miles helped me **focusing on the pains we want to solve**, defining the solution we can provide, analyzing the **market size** & designing a **great pitch**.

This program brought me also **visibility**, as there were communications on it, and on the ideas developed. It also gave me more confidence & liberty in my choices. I always have in mind the moto we had during this 4 months, which is that "**you don't get what you don't ask**".

Why this business could not have been developed through the traditional system?

It's not only about technology: even if technology is key to set-up this marketplace but, as you are creating something new, it's all about **users & change management**, and working with the spirit of the lean startup methodology gives the place for creation, innovation & iteration.

What are the key figures that you would like to share about your business?

18 months ago (mid-2018), we started with an idea, and today we are a team of **10 people** working on this product, delivering its 1st version, with **hundreds of users, hundreds of thousands of products** proposed, and 1st transactions on going.

Still a lot of challenges to address to confirm it can fly, and with the desire to act for the good of planet which is our key driver.

What learnings would you like to share with fledgling intrapreneurs?

- Work hard to really **understand the problem** you want to solve, it's key!
- Give **sense** to your activity, you are building cathedrals!
- **Act, fail, learn & act again;**
- And don't forget that you don't get what you don't ask ! **Don't be afraid**.

Engie: Christophe Huguet, Nextflex (engie-nextflex.com/)

In March 2016, Engie presented the first 5 new businesses incubated internally and developed by employees, including NextFlex. Its creator, Christophe Huguet, an expert in energy business with over 20 years of experience, has been a long way since then. Christophe, a seasoned employee, explains how intrapreneurship **turned him into a startup leader, going beyond his own limits, and experiencing the best of 2 worlds: corporate and startup.**

What is the business of your corporate startup? Did the intrapreneur project transition to a corporate business line, or a spin-out startup?

Our business is the **monetization of electrical flexibility** (Demand vs Response). We pay industrial and tertiary sites for the service they provide us to adapt their electricity consumption to our demand. In less than 2 hours, we lower the electrical consumption of the industrial site, and monetize the unused capacity with electricity operators.

After the intrapreneurship phase, we **joined an Engie business unit**.

How did the program for intrapreneurs help you? At the project level, and the personal development level?

The program helped me in two ways:

- At the project level because the changeover to the **"startup" mode** of operation, and the **involvement of project sponsors** made it possible to make it emerge, and accelerate its development;
- At a personal level because the **miscellaneous coaching** allowed a change of mindset and methods that were decisive for the success of the project. I was advised on how to recruit and retain my team, develop my commercial capabilities, and gradually acquire the makings of **a true startup boss**.

In the beginning, you limit yourself, you sometimes lack self-confidence. Thanks to the incubation, we gain assurance.

Why this business could not have been developed through the traditional system?

The processes of a large company like Engie, and especially the processes of risk assessment and decision-making, are unsuitable for **some new and small businesses**. It is more effective to get out of this framework to move forward, than to want to change it, and come back when you can prove that the project / business was viable.

What are the key figures that you would like to share about your business?

After 5 years, our turnover is of **12 M€**. We value the flexibility of nearly **300 sites** in France, Belgium and Holland.

What learnings would you like to share with fledgling intrapreneurs?

Intrapreneurship allows choosing **the best of two worlds**: corporate and startup. It combines the freedom to undertake, to take risks, without necessarily having a lot of visibility, and the possibility of relying on Engie's expertise, networks, distribution capacities.

It lets you also **hack the rules** that are not suitable. Do not forget it, and do not miss this license.

La Poste: Isabelle Legrand and Sandra Beraudo, Kidscare

Isabelle Legrand joined Docapost (La Poste group) 30 years ago where she developed multiple IT programs. Sandra Beraudo is Responsible of Docapost Sophia-Antipolis Center since 2010. They both team up to build an app for schools ecosystem that became **a new business unit, and a subsidiary of their corporation.**

What is the business of your corporate startup? Did the intrapreneur project transition to a corporate business line, or a spin-out startup?

KidsCare is a web and mobile application that has been completely developed by a 100% KidsCare team. This application is intended for town halls, schools and parents, but also activity clubs.

It improves **communication between the different players (town halls, schools and parents), and contributes to the safety of children.**

KidsCare is a **100% subsidiary** of La Poste Intrapreneuriat.

The CEO is a representative from La Poste, and Sandra and I are Deputy Directors but we do not appear on the commercial registry form (Kbis).

How did the program for intrapreneurs help you? At the project level, and the personal development level?

Setting up such a project in a group like La Poste is an undeniable advantage. We can rely on **group resources** that help us a lot.

Why this business could not have been developed through the traditional system?

It probably could have emerged in the traditional system but we probably would never have launched. The **risk** would have been too great. We would not have taken it.

What are the key figures that you would like to share about your business?

We are a firm of 9 people who work 100% for KidsCare.

After 10 months of activity (the company was created in 2018 December 21) we have more than **10,000 users**.

What learnings would you like to share with fledgling intrapreneurs?

With intrapreneurship, we can rely on the resources of the company and it is HUGE.

We learn a lot, every day.

We never get bored. We are motivated as ever!

Malakoff Médéric: Jean-Baptiste Richardet and Jérémy Marlin, Cameo (cameo.fr)

Jean-Baptiste Richardet and Jérémy Martin are respectively CTO and CEO, and the young Co-Founders of Cameo, a first output of Malakoff Médéric program for intrapreneurs. Jean-Baptiste joined Malakoff in 2017, and Jérémy in 2012. They illustrate how intrapreneurship can combine **employees with different seniority** in the company, and let them explore a new market **testing their offerings with their sponsors as customers**, and scaling through a **spin-out** which counts the corporation as stakeholder.

What is the business of your corporate startup? Did the intrapreneur project transition to a corporate business line, or a spin-out startup?

Cameo's goal is to create **a new kind of training for employees**: experience first-hand the life of an executive in an innovative small business. During 3 months, you will live a meaningful adventure helping a positive-impact startup with your skills and experience. At the same time, they will teach you new methods, new tools and a new meaning.

When you come back, your goal will be to set up in your organization an innovation you learned during your Cameo mission. It addresses all the issues around internal mobility, GPEC and bottom-up innovation.

As this was not aligned with Malakoff Médéric core business (health insurance), we decided to create a spin-out but **Malakoff Médéric still choose to fund our seed round**.

How did the program for intrapreneurs help you? At the project level, and the personal development level?

Being intrapreneurs allowed us to access **external resources like mentoring, legal expertise and market sizing**.

It also created a direct **contact with MM's board**, especially with the HR, Sales and Innovation Directors, who challenged us monthly, still follow our accomplishment and guide us in moments of doubt. As they represent **our persona**, the project greatly benefits from their inputs.

On a personal level, it trained us to **speak with high level director** and give us a bunch of experience in negotiation with a board.

Moreover, from now on, we no longer wait for orders from above, but thrive on **self-initiative**; we try, test, fail and try again until success is met, even if we have to do it ourselves!

Why this business could not have been developed through the traditional system?

As said before, our business was **on the rim of MM business**, so we wouldn't have any fund to create a team with a traditional system. Also, we had to move fast (the market is new and will soon attract big companies) and freely (fail fast, lean and prototyping) which is not how new projects emerged traditionally.

What are the key figures that you would like to share about your business?

After 6 months (Cameo was created in April), we already convinced **10 CAC40 companies** planning to send up to 5 people each in startups in 2020.

Due to the new legislation around AFEST ("learning by doing") we're often invited in conference and round tables to explain and discuss it.

But our pride is in our **contract with the CFDT union**, which will train long time elected member who lost their seat. 2020 will be a challenge!

What learnings would you like to share with fledgling intrapreneurs?

It's all about politics! **Find the key people** who can help your project develop with resources (funds, people, network) and pitch them, frequently. If they find an interest in your project, it's a win.

And until you find such a person, **keep the moral up** with sports, drinks with your team and sleep. Remember that if you burn out, your project dies with you, so **don't overpush yourself**, sometimes a bit of rest is better than an implosion.

makesense: Lucy Chartouny, Paumé.e.s (makesense.org/paume-e-s/)

Lucy Chartouny works at makesense as community developer and trainer in community building for corporates (Vinci, Orange, SETC) and coach for startups (Red Cress, and other companies with social impact). Makesense supports citizens, entrepreneurs, and organizations in sparking communities and programs with a societal impact.

Lucy is one of the co-founder of Paumé.e.s community, an intrapreneurs' project within makesense [Paumé.e.s means feeling like you lost the clue, confused]. Lucy demonstrates how to start an intrapreneur project without the support of a dedicated program, but with the benefit of a **pervading intrapreneurial culture in the organization**.

What is the business of your corporate startup? Did the intrapreneur project transition to a corporate business line, or to a spin-out startup?

Paumé.e.s is a showcase of what the makesense association best know-how: **engaging young people in causes that matter** to them. It's a new activity within makesense association. Paumé.e.s is a community of young people who are committed to the quest for professional and personal meaning.

160

Paumé.es business model does not rely on monetizing the community: it's about creating knowledge. Learning from our experience allows us to better understand the expectations of young workers at work. Makesense offers range from skills sponsorship, intrapreneurship, internal corporate communities, but also new modes of governance, and they address HR issues, and the transformation of the company from the inside, by or for young people.

How did the program for intrapreneurs help you? At the project level, and the personal development level?

We did benefit from an informal intrapreneurial program as intrapreneurship is part of makesense culture: many advisers and helpers accompanied us in structuring the project.

A quarterly advisory board allowed us to monitor progress, and set ourselves clear goals and KPIs. The feedback from this board has also been invaluable in connecting with other makesense activities, and ensuring that we are following the common course.

We gave away some project developments (for example some organized events) because they did not support the reason why of makesense (recruit, train and accompany the move to action of event organizers). We also completed our team with **a new profile** in charge of "partnerships" which was not with us initially. The advisory board pushed us constantly, and worked with us so that Paumé.e.s could develop over time.

Our time spent on the project has evolved over time: it was initially a project handled "in addition" to our daily work; today the **sum of time allocated to the subject arises to a full time**.

Why this business could not have been developed through the traditional system?

Paumé.es began with a podcast, born from the desire of Aurore, co-initiator of the project, and completely **aside of existing business**: makesense did not have any podcast activity. Paumé.e.s tone of voice, with quirky spirit and humor, derives also from our own desires. We did not necessarily find this particular leeway or **freedom** of speech in our daily activities.

What are the key figures that you would like to share about your business?

In one year podcasts were played 67,000 times, **80 events were organized by community members gathering 2,500 people**; 7,000 people belong to the main online group, and several regional subgroups have arisen.

A very rich press coverage, with articles in Le Monde and Les Echos, or TV reports in France 2 and LCI, has echoed the initiative.

What learnings would you like to share with fledgling intrapreneurs?

Go ahead if you believe in it, and you have the intuition that there is untapped potential!

As co-founders of paumé.e.s we had all been through phases of cluelessness, and regretted at the time that there was no space to interact with people who feel the same. **We experienced the problem that we were willing to solve.** It has not always been easy (additional workload, sometimes a feeling of giving a lot, and being constantly challenged in return) but I have never been **happier in my job** and **fulfilled** than since I took part in this project.

Orange: Vincent Philippe, Cobiz (cobiz.orange-business.com)

In 2017, Vincent Philippe, a marketer at the Orange Business Services (OBS) Connectivity business unit, joined Orange Intrapreneurs Studio, Orange program for intrapreneurs, to develop his innovation project, Cobiz. Cobiz illustrates that **innovation is not limited to new product and service**, and that it can relate to **distribution channel, and business model**.

What is the business of your corporate startup? Did the intrapreneur project transition to a corporate business line, or to a spin-out startup?

Cobiz is a platform that **brings together Orange Business Services sales forces and local digital services companies**. The platform allows them to work together to make proposals for corporate client projects (small businesses customer segment).

Based on the proofs of value provided during the incubation phase and the future prospects of the project, the director of Customer Marketing & Innovation (CMI) at Orange Business Services, decided in 2019 to upscale Cobiz by incorporating it into her entity. This is how Cobiz ended up joining the CMI innovation team.

Where did you get the idea for your Cobiz project?

The idea came to me in late 2016 while designing a new security service. I was contacted by the Value Team Board – an OBS governance entity allowing employees to pitch their projects to Business Unit directors. I presented my business model with a value proposal and a new sales approach for the middle market (small businesses customer segment). They liked my proposal and challenged me on the hypotheses of my business model.

Then over three months, I **conducted interviews** with the local IT teams, and our sales force to obtain approval.

They then offered me the chance to work full time on Cobiz and to take the lead on my own initiative.

How did the program for intrapreneurs help you? At the project level, and the personal development level?

I was advised to enter the competition for the pilot season of this new incubation program, the Intrapreneurs Studio. I was one of the three lucky winners of the competition. I joined the Intrapreneurs Studio in June 2017 and started conducting the first experiments for my project.

The Intrapreneurs Studio provided me with **governance, sponsors, and great opportunities for rewarding discussions with other project teams**. They also provided **financial support**, with a half-yearly budget paid according to the objectives and stages of the project. I also worked with an **agile coach** to set up my team during the initial development phase of the Cobiz platform.

The methodology was mainly inspired by **design thinking, agility and lean startup**, with 'problem solution fit' and 'product market fit' approaches.

In the beginning, there were three of us working with phones and post-it notes, sort of like a **'concierge' service**. We connected OBS sales representatives from two test corporate branches with local partners, selected on the needs of the branch and the client projects.

Once I obtained validation that my proposal addressed the problem, and established mechanisms for the users, my team and I began to think about how to digitalize the solution and turn it into a platform.

What are the key figures that you would like to share about your business?

Cobiz has already handled around **a hundred cases** from the OBS sales force. Around forty sales have been made thanks to Cobiz, with an incremental sales figure of € 300,000.

We also have various user testimonials from within and outside the company describing how the service has gained **traction,** and even gone **viral.**

Customer feedback has led to a change in the packaging of offers giving **a competitive advantage to the Orange cloud**

What learnings would you like to share with fledgling intrapreneurs?

Innovation isn't an aim in itself. It's a means to improve performance (revenue, costs, and lead-times) and strategy. The most effective innovations in recent times have dealt with **business models** rather than technology.

You need to **get in touch with the client** ("get out of the building"), and the business units as soon as possible to test your hypotheses, and update your business model.

This is an eye-catching enabler to put together **a network of allies**, and a team of contributors to the initiative, and provide a strong sense of commitment.

Orange Guinée: Mohamed Lamine Keita, Feinteingni

Mohamed Lamine Keita has been working on Digital, CSR, and Branding for 8 years at Orange Guinée. He was promoted to head HR internal communication division, consequently to his successful selection by the intrapreneur jury: obviously Mohamed demonstrates how intrapreneurship can **accelerate your career**!

Moreover, Mohamed project is a smart combination of how to **explore a new market while making use of key assets in the company**: when an incumbent becomes a new entrant.

What is the business of your corporate startup? Did the intrapreneur project transition to a corporate business line, or a spin-out startup?

Our project is called "Orange Feinteingni": Feinteingni means cleanliness in one of the Guinean local languages. It is an **intermediation platform** between waste collectors (SMEs) and families. The idea came following a customer survey, showing a crisis of confidence between waste collectors and their customers, some facing collection and payment problems, and others with difficulties in evacuating their household waste.

The Orange Feinteingni platform will make it possible, thanks to a mobile application, to offer an **online payment solution via Orange Money**, and to identify, through connected sensors, all the bins that need to be collected at the customers' premises in order to optimize the pick-up journey. The bins connected sensors will send a signal to collectors once filled.

This application will be part of the **portfolio of Orange Guinea offers**, corresponding to the diversification of its activities to be a multiservices operator, and to offer other types of services than telecom to its customers.

How did the program for intrapreneurs help you? At the project level, and the personal development level?

The program for intrapreneurs allowed me to discover the "**Lean Startup**" method, where everything is **tested** with end users to propose a solution that caters their needs precisely.

From the beginning of the project, we had **trainings and a permanent coaching** of the Intrapreneurs Studio which allowed us to refine the project, and to give it a better orientation and presentation for the qualification phase.

So, from the preparation of the pitch, until the day of the presentation, I was able to acquire a lot of experience and especially to develop my **speaking abilities** in public.

After the selection, we participated in a very insightful boot sprint: 3 days at Okoni Fab Lab to **materialize our concept with visuals** (mobile user interface, mood board, video of us acting as ours target users,...), and **prototype** a connected bin.

Until then, I had never had any experience of conducting this type of project: it has become a reality today, since we have taken important steps that will lead to its completion.

Why this business could not have been developed through the traditional system?

This project would have been difficult to achieve if it had not been supported by the Intrapreneurs Studio through its coaching system for candidates, and sponsored by Orange Guinée through one of its Business Units.

What are the key figures that you would like to share about your business?

During the process, we worked on a business plan that should lead to the following results:

- 5,000 buildings connected to the solution in one of the communes of the capital city;
- **30,000 families subscribing to the service**;
- An income of 5,400,000 GNF (540,000 €) from commissions over one year, through the payments completed by the families on the platform;

- An income of 500,000,000 GNF (50,000 €) from the installation costs of garbage cans in buildings.

What learnings would you like to share with fledgling intrapreneurs?

Intrapreneurship is a unique experience because it allowed me, as an employee to discover a new world, that of entrepreneurship. It took me **out of my comfort zone** and made me practice a new way of working.

In just a few months, I learned how to set up a project, **test it with users**, use feedback to refine the project, carry out field surveys, draw up a business plan, promotional video spots, complete a good pitch, etc.

It also helps **creativity,** and allows me to feel **a key asset to the company**, especially if the project achieves expected results.

Radio France: Adeline Beving / Aurélie Kieffer, Emilie Gautreau, Justine Dibling, La Chouette Radio

Adeline Beving is Deputy Director of Innovation at Radio France, which she joined 9 years ago. She loves to promote innovative and creative ideas, and that's what she did with the team of La Chouette Radio composed of Aurélie Kieffer, Emilie Gautreau, and Justine Dibling. Adeline tells us how **intrapreneurship can take the corporation to new digital service & device, and propose a framework for cross-entities project.**

What is the business of your corporate startup? Did the intrapreneur project transition to a corporate business line, or a spin-out startup?

La Chouette Radio is basically **a radio for young children aged 3 to 9.** It is a three-fold project including audio content for kids, an app for parents to program the content according to their daily schedule, and a connected listening device that children can carry around.

The project has passed the prototype phase and its actual feasibility and implementation plan is currently under review.

How did the program for intrapreneurs help you? At the project level, and the personal development level?

The intrapreneurs program helped us **transform a mere idea into an actual product**. It provided us with the **methodology, environment and resources** we needed to make progress.

The very project team originated in the program's requirement of gathering employees from diverse backgrounds.

At a personal level it enhanced our understanding of the **digital culture**, strengthened our user centric approach, and actually gave **a second wind to our professional motivation**.

Why this business could not have been developed through the traditional system?

The idea was too disruptive to find room in the non stop daily workflow of a radio station.

Besides, young children were not considered as a priority target audience before the program was launched.

Last but not least, La Chouette Radio is based on gathering skills and resources **transverse** to the whole of Radio France, which is quite unusual for a company that is structurally compartmented into 7 different channels.

What are the key figures that you would like to share about your business?

- **100% of test users** think La chouette radio is a great gift to offer a kid;

173

- 15% of French households include children aged 3-9;
- Radio France podcasts listening curve jumped from 15M/month in 2014 to 75M/month today (x5).

What learnings would you like to share with fledgling intrapreneurs?

Welcome questioning but hold on to your deepest convictions.

Never give up, even when the project seems to linger.

Never take no for an answer, however shy you feel about asking again.

RATP: Benjamin Charles, AMY

Having worked at RATP for 10 years, with very operational responsibilities (management of 180 subways drivers, Tramway operations, and troubles reporting), Benjamin Charles joined the program for intrapreneurs in may 2019 to create AMY. Benjamin **opened a new service line** for his company, **adopted intrapreneur's role, and upgraded his skills to manage a digital device,** taking the most of various innovation programs, and learning how to deal with the unexpected.

What is the business of your corporate startup? Did the intrapreneur project transition to a corporate business line, or a spin-out startup?

AM is a digital and innovative solution that uses **ultrasound technology to save the lives of pedestrians fascinated by their smartphones** (specifically "smombies" a new word formed from smartphone and zombie, because it is true that one quickly looks like a zombie when you're stuck on your phone in the street!).

AMY is primarily aimed at transport operators and mobility authorities, and includes:

- Selling and setting-up a transmitter device for vehicles / infrastructures, and SDK for smartphones;
- License to use the technological device;

- Maintenance and system evolutions;
- Data usage reporting.

It's free for the pedestrian who benefits from this service (just like for the applications developers or telco operators who want to integrate this functionality).

I am currently managing this project, full time since 4 months (the project was born 2.5 years ago). **AMY SA, a subsidiary of RATP Participations**, should be settled by the end of the year.

How did the program for intrapreneurs help you? At the project level, and the personal development level?

For 4 months, I benefited from the RATP participative innovation program BOUGE (support provided by Numa) at the birth of AMY in January 2017. I learned **new ways of working**, and I especially went beyond the traditional framework of my company (RATP): very rewarding both professionally and personally.

I was later accompanied by Capgemini especially for the formalization of my Business Plan (December 2018).

At the same time I joined the RATP SMART program on another topic, which allowed me to take advantage of this new support also on AMY.

Engineer graduate and having been mainly in operational positions since the beginning of my career, I developed **new skills (financial, art pitch, ...)** and another way of seeing things. And especially now, **I dare** (especially when I'm told it's not possible!).

Why this business could not have been developed through the traditional system?

For 2 reasons:

- It was necessary to **go quickly** to put this product on the market because the "smombies" topic began to get awareness, and that it was necessary to preserve this competitive advance (traditional project management methods did not allow to go so quickly);
- We had to be able to reach a market outside of the company and create **a new line of business** (orientation decided by our CEO), and from the start, to collect the expectations of future customers (type SNCF).

What are the key figures that you would like to share about your business?

AMY is in the pre-industrialization phase thanks to a major **in-house fundraising** completed in May. It has already been successfully **tested on buses and trams** as well as on a **railroad crossing** of SNCF.

The media coverage has been immediate, each time the device was presented (at the Vivatech show, a report on AMY was broadcasted on M6 channel newscast as well as on BFM radio).

- M6 Newscast: https://www.youtube.com/watch?v=AWbL0T_EgIM
- BFM: https://m.youtube.com/watch?v=_IEVkw3aVqI&feature=youtu.be

What learnings would you like to share with fledgling intrapreneurs?

Recently, a member of my company's COMEX who follows the project closely told me: "It's really an asset for you to be an ultra trail rider to carry out this project." Indeed it is not at all wrong (which does not mean that you must necessarily make the ultra trail to be intrapreneur ;-)) as there are 2 similarities:

- The road is **very long** to reach the end of the intrapreneurs project;
- We think we are prepared for everything, and yet very often, we are confronted with a multitude of **unexpected events** that can affect motivation;

Sometimes we can **feel really alone** and it is especially at these moments that we should not hesitate to exchange with those who live the same thing: knowing that we are not alone in difficulty does a lot of good, and there is no competition with other intrapreneurs!

You may think you have reached a peak at the end of a long and painful climb and once there, **surprise**: there is another summit which seems insurmountable to cross! But the more one crosses, and the more you're prepared to cross new summits.

Despite the difficulties, **never give up**, and tell yourself that the difficult times will give way to great moments of happiness of fulfillment.

Once we have reached the end, we only retain the positive, and we have only one desire: **keep on going, and start again**!

SNCF Mobilités: Anne-Sophie Nomblot, Eco-Store (laboutiqueeco.sncf.fr/)

Anne-Sophie Nomblot is Innovation and Development Manager for the Paris region stations and Entrepreneur in Sustainable Development. In the continuity of a 15 years' experience in operational and management at SNCF, she implements innovative shops, and services in the stations of the Paris region. Anne-Sophie unearthed **a new business model, taking advantage of underutilized assets, and creating a societal impact.**

What is the business of your corporate startup? Did the intrapreneur project transition to a corporate business line, or a spin-out startup?

The project we carried out impacts sustainable development: it's a website that allows you to **give in-house professional material that is not used anymore**. This project has been reintegrated into the business, under the responsibility of the **purchasing department**. Financing was found very quickly from different directions (Sustainable development, purchasing ...).

How did the program for intrapreneurs help you? At the project level, and the personal development level?

The program was essential to initiate, and **launch the project**: training, networking, support, acculturation to the world of startups were key. I still use today training modules in my daily job (how to pitch ....). More broadly it gave me confidence in **daring to push my projects**.

Why this business could not have been developed through the traditional system?

The project was **too transversal**, it involved many directions. The traditional system could not allow pushing it quickly.

What are the key figures that you would like to share about your business?

In 12 months we acquired more than **10,000 users** and **saved 200 000 € in 12 months, and 300 000 € since June 2019** thanks to the Eco Store.

What learnings would you like to share with fledgling intrapreneurs?

I think the key is to talk about the project around you, in order to have feedback, contacts and ultimately **a community that supports you**, and promote the project.

Société Générale: Yaël Dehaese, IT4girls (@IT_4_Girls, linkedin.com/in/yaeldehaese)

Yaël Dehaese joined Société Générale 15 years ago, handling successive marketing and communication responsibilities. She's now Project Manager for Change - promoting mixity at IT departments of Société Générale, and a scrappy intrapreneur for IT4Girls. Yaël explains how **her company became the first customer of her startup, how it helped open the doors of other big companies, and how she leverages the communication expertise acquired as an employee in her new business**.

What is the business of your corporate startup? Did the intrapreneur project transition to a corporate business line, or a spin-out startup?

IT4Girls is a program that offers **coding workshops for the children of employees** (especially girls since we target 50 to 100% of girls in our workshops) but also **for women**, working in the company, who would like to raise awareness about programming. The spirit of these workshops is co-creation, playing at environmental or species protection games, for a better future.

The goal is to improve, in the more or less long term, the number of women in IT services by proving concretely that computers have no gender!

IT4girls **startup** is now independent, it has its own structure, however the company where she was born became a client.

How did the program for intrapreneurs help you? At the project level, and the personal development level?

The assistance provided by the program has been crucial. As Project Manager and Communication Officer for many years, I knew how to manage a project, communicate on social networks and other media and put forward my project. However, I had to acquire **skills in strategy, finance, team management in agile mode, and ... coding**!

From a personal point of view, I went **from employee to entrepreneur** and... it changes everything: more leadership, more ambition, more determination, among others!

Why this business could not have been developed through the traditional system?

Actually, it could have been!

Having a strong link with my company (being an internal project at the beginning) **opened the doors of other big companies** that had the same problems and became my clients. I am from a large group, I speak the same language, adopt the same codes and references as my potential clients.

What are the key figures that you would like to share about your business?

By the time we started the startup project, we had only really done one workshop. We are **over 100 workshops** today. We had the idea before the track record but that did not stop us from moving forward.

Our goal was to train between 50 and 100% girls per workshop. We have an average of **70% girls per workshop**, and are very proud of it.

We have barely a year of existence and will achieve an annual turnover of K€ 100 this year by having trained more than 1000 people! Basically, **we skyrocketed our KPIs**, and we did not even imagine it!

What learnings would you like to share with fledgling intrapreneurs?

Believe in one's project; **do not hesitate to meet other entrepreneurs** even if they are potential competitors.

Share a maximum of information, rather than keeping it to yourself, listen to your customer, address his request, adapt as quickly as possible.

And finally: **spam social networks** (LinkedIn) regularly and outrageously. ☺

https://youtu.be/AOxEe6RiCxs

https://www.challenges.fr/femmes/la-start-up-it4girls-veut-eveiller-les-filles-aux-metiers-du-numerique_611964

Thales: Jean-Yves Ingea, Heropolis (heropolis.fr)

Jean-Yves Ingea is CEO at Heropolis, a spin-off of Thales Group, unearthed in 2015. Previously he worked for 11 years at Thales Communications as Workpackage Manager, and then Bid Support Manager. Jean-Yves shares with us **the building of his team of "chameleons employees", and how he reaped benefits from the corporate accelerator** for internal projects.

What is the business of your corporate startup? Did the intrapreneur project transition to a corporate business line, or a spin-out startup?

Our startup has changed **from an internal startup to a spin-out**, and autonomous company which was **co-founded by the team and Thales**.

We are producing a new way of **managing safety**, security, and emergency for organizations, cities and large companies, thanks to enriched and secure alerts mechanisms combining mobile app, connected devices, and a SaaS application.

How did the program for intrapreneurs help you? At the project level, and the personal development level?

Our intrapreneurship program has started with a 54 hours event. This event allowed us to **gather the team** (3 of them are now the startup co-founders), create a first pitch, and meet our first internal investors.

Coaches and workshops before, during and after this event have changed us from the usual corporate mindset to a more **innovative and open-minded creative mindset.**

At this point, we had started to become "**chameleons employees**", able more and more to think and behave in a different way than only acting our job in the company: from developers, project managers, system engineers, we became product owners, business developers, marketers, UX designers, etc, and connected more and more to other specialists and entities within the company : jurists, product line managers, heads of business lines, etc.

Then the second part of that program happened for us: to be **accelerated at the Thales Digital Factory**. At that time, we were working full time to the project, and preparing the spin-off process. We became fund-raisers, accountants, creating, and developing our brand, specific values, and culture.

Why this business could not have been developed through the traditional system?

The way we are selling the product, the way we quickly needed the resources to grow (buying stuff, developing in a lighter process), the market we were first addressing (small cities) was **unusual for the company**.

We didn't know it at that time, but the Thales top management was aware of it, and we had a frank exchange with them about these pain points, and together, we took the right decision to step further to a spin-off startup.

What are the key figures that you would like to share about your business?

My 2 first customers, and early adopters! Loiret (French department) and the city of Anould in the Vosges area.

Some human figures were essential:

- First, the CreateRocks company members, who run the first internal innovation event : Raphaël Thobie, and his team;
- Then some key managers in the company that helped us for resources and strategy : Gérard Herby (VP protection system), André Méchaly (Digital Marketing director);
- The step after, people from Thales Digital Factory : Olivier Flous (head of the Factory) and Jean-Yves Plu (leading the startup program at the Factory);
- And until now, coaches from Thales still beside us : Hamilton Mann (digital marketing group director) and Marie-Laure Miglietti (digital value coach).

What learnings would you like to share with fledgling intrapreneurs?

Become again a student and stay humble, and at the same time be confident, and faithful with your project. Good coaches and a good network are crucial for you and for your business.

Things will probably take much more time than what you think.

Total: Claire Le Louët, Kleen (kleen-now.com/)

Claire Le Louët is Head of Business Acceleration at Total Marketing Services. She was directly involved in the intrapreneur project, Kleen, and explains how **combining lead intrapreneur with corporate startups studio** expertise proved to be nifty collaboration. The output resulted in **an affiliate, and the design of a digital service** to the greatest benefit of the end-user.

What is the business of your corporate startup? Did the intrapreneur project transition to a corporate business line, or a spin-out startup?

Kleen is an intrapreneurial project: we created the **1st marketplace in the car wash** segment.

Nobody has to go to a cashier anymore! Thanks to the app, you select, pay and drive-in directly to the wash lane, thanks to a geolocalized offer valid for a month, in over 1,300 car-washes located in France.

At the beginning, we were an internal digital project. After 9 months of intensive market study and preliminary work, we decided to excubate ourselves from our digital department to an incubator located in Paris center. 6 months later we created the venture, an **affiliate** of our Big Corp.

How did the intrapreneurs program help you? At the project level, and the personal development level?

Thanks to the **startups studio** intrapreneurial structure, we had the utmost chance to benefit from **initial funds, empathy, support from sponsors and internal experts** to navigate into this hybrid world of acting as a start-upper into the Big Corp world.

We were lucky also to **team up with consultants** at the very beginning as there were only 1 lead intrapreneur in the team!

Definitely, founding a start-up is hard work place where time flies as fast as your to-do-list piles up in fields one would never have thought off! **Multidisciplinarity, trust, confidence, speed, maker spirit, team player** are core basics.

On a personal side, it has been **very demanding**. Some think intrapreneurship are holidays. They are WRONG. Like any entrepreneur, racing in this start-up world is thrilling, you go through ups and downs, and long hours. Family time shrinks at the same speed as it becomes a family business!

The game is worth it though: never ever before, you feel yourself as useful and **self-accomplishing** as during this magic intrapreneurial time.

Why this business could not have been developed through the traditional system?

190

Our carwash offer at that time was not **digital**, nor did we were data oriented. Neither marketplace nor drive to store had been tested. **Agility** was a word not a reality. So it was a revolution per se! Worst, we have been challenged everyday as we were seen as competitors despite our internal explanations of addressing a new client base.

Finally, to comply with competition issues, it was safer to be excubated.

What are the key figures that you would like to share about your business?

- **110,000 clients** got our app.
- After 3 years of operations, the team consisted of 10 bright talents. We have been incorporated back in our Big Corp business line with a massive marketing ambition to offer new digital services in the car wash service.

What learnings would you like to share with fledgling intrapreneurs?

- Don't wait to be ready to start;
- **Prepare yourself,** and your family for this life adventure;
- Be organized ahead up until when you are action driven only!
- Keep your **mentors** in your closed circle;
- Please the **client,** always.

Total: Leo Nwofa, TURN – Total Unitar Recycling Nigeria

Leo Nwofa joined Total Nigeria 7 years ago as Technical Service and Development Engineer, working on product development & customer service. As an intrapreneur, he is Plastic Recycling & Circular Economy Manager. He exhibits how **an intrapreneur can bring an idea, validate the concept, set the pilot on tracks, and transfer to an external entrepreneur to scale-up the adventure**.

What is the business of your corporate startup?

We process **plastic recycling** and regeneration of post-consumer Polyethylene and Polypropylene resins.

By 2050, if nothing is done, it is estimated that there will be **more plastics than fish in the world's oceans!** Our vision therefore is to facilitate sustainable waste management in Africa (starting from Nigeria) through empowerment of local ecosystem in creating **a sustainable plastic recycling circular economy**, as a highlight of Total's values and commitment to humanity.

The recycling plant is a pilot, first of its kind to be used as a so called TRIC (Training, Research and Information Center). It shall illustrate a sustainable circular economic model while creating jobs, and reducing environmental footprint.

The model involves **monetary incentive** to plastic waste aggregators, manual sorting of collected plastics (scraps), automated grinding, washing and pelletizing of regenerated plastics. The regenerated resins are then sold to plastic converters for various applications including, housewares, hangers, containers, furniture and others. The product will substitute exports, reduce dependency on foreign exchange, and would be over **40% cheaper** than virgin resin.

High quality recycled resins are in short supply in Nigeria today, and our product is targeted to fill in the gap. If model proves viable, it will be transferred to other entrepreneurs, organizations or governments for duplication and expansion.

Did the intrapreneur project transition to a corporate business line, or a spin-out startup?

Yes it did, the aim is to **empower an external entrepreneur to start a spin-off** which the project has achieved. We did set up list of criteria like, he/she must be active in the value chain, be in alignment to the vision, local, passion and hunger to make a difference while being business minded. During my study I met many people who are then interviewed and screened together with UNITAR (United Nations Institute of Training And Research).

The facility is yet to be constructed but currently it is at the design stage, where various factors are being taken into consideration amongst all HSE (Health, Safety and

Environment) which is a core value for Total. Safety is KEY. Based on the project schedule **the plant is projected to start up end Q1 2020** to be managed by the selected entrepreneur under the supervision and guidance of Total and UNITAR. The spin-off will also serve as a learning avenue for Total polymer division to explore potential business opportunities in the future within the nation/continent .

How did the program for intrapreneurs help you? At the project level, and the personal development level?

Actually I never followed the "program for intrapreneurs" but was privileged to undergo training and coaching of **Total Innovation accelerator** program by "**Booster**".

At the project level, it helped me **streamline the various pieces of puzzles**, and hence gain direction and focus.

Secondly, it taught me how to identify, understand and engage **stakeholders** which has been instrumental. Ideas structuring, and putting together a convincing presentation for sponsors and stakeholders is an important outcome from the training. An illustrative structure would be Pains, Why/Challenge, Solution, and Stakeholders & Benefits.

On a personal development level, it has been an **eye opener** and has given **invaluable exposure**. My interpersonal relationships, **communication** and time management skills have greatly improved. Ability to see things from various perspectives, **think outside of the box,** and approach challenges with an open mind, have become a part of me.

Why this business could not have been developed through the traditional system?

As innovative and pioneering as Total is, it's a multinational company with sheer magnitude that could be likened to **a big ship**, not easy to maneuver, and definitely can't dock at every harbor, nor sail close to the shore.

This limits its agility and ability to reach some terrains, manage small businesses, take dynamic decisions needed for small enterprises to be created sustainably. Also as a big ship, it carries huge overhead both in cost and administration. Other important reasons would be **risk management**, exposure to local community and political barriers.

The project has gained grounds within the group as it **aligns greatly with Total's vision** and ambition of becoming a world-class energy company that:

- Contributes to the development of growing population by providing affordable energy;
- Is helping to address the challenges of climate change and;
- Is in tune with its customers' changing needs.

What are the key figures that you would like to share about your business?

- **Recycling capacity of 800 tons yearly - equivalent to 130 African bush Elephants**;
- **CO_2 reduction of over 550 tons per year** ;
- To generate more than **20 direct jobs** the first year; and over 100 indirect jobs;
- Will train minimum 15 entrepreneurs per year;
- Over 20 million tons per annum of plastics end up in the oceans (55kt/d > 2000trucks) ~6% global consumption;
  - Roughly 80% of plastics in the ocean comes from land;
  - Polyethylene and Polypropylene both make up the largest portion of global plastics – over 60%.

What learnings would you like to share with fledgling intrapreneurs?

- **BE SIMPLE**;
- **Build project in stages**, split into small chewable chunks;
- **Engage** management and colleagues;
- **Sell** sell sell and when sold, sell again!
- Innovative **out of the box** thinking, and **challenge the status quo**;
- Maintain **visibility** at all times; and share your ideas;
- **Passion, and determination** are vital fuel to keep you going;

- **Locate project champion(s**) within your organization and entities: those are decision makers/influential people within the organization, who will give you higher visibility, be your voice where you can't reach or access someone, pressure management when needed, utterly give the project weight. They can be middle or higher management;
- Endless possibilities if **open minded, assertive and possess a never say never attitude.**

Conclusion

Intrapreneurship is a powerful and sustainable tool to create new business lines, and foster personal development of employees. Moreover it's a global agent of change, as intrapreneurs impact many colleagues in the course of their project. The intrapreneur skill set covers innovation project management, team management, networking, and developing a network of allies: **intrapreneurship is a school of leadership**, and it hasn't scratched the surface of its potential yet.

The societal dimension resonates perfectly with intrapreneurship: it increases even more the intrapreneur determination. Obviously encouraging intrapreneurship with a societal impact must be on the same page with the corporation strategy, and tangible engagements.

In a nutshell, **intrapreneurship can result in an astonishing alchemy between innovation, human experience, and societal impact.**

But intrapreneurship is subject to **tricky conditions** to succeed: the persistent support of C-level sponsors, the commitment of business units, the coaching with scrutiny of intrapreneurs, along with tight schedules, fostering a creative tension, are paramount. Among the coaching levers, exposing intrapreneurs to entrepreneurs on a regular basis can help intrapreneurs keep the fast-track path.

When these conditions are met, **intrapreneurship can scale**!

Intrapreneurship complements effortlessly the various types of Innovation Labs archetypes. Pioneering companies are paving the way forward by combining them: Vinci Leonard mingles intrapreneurship, open innovation, prospective, and cross-BUs projects, while Total hosts intrapreneurs selected in his startups studio.

What makes sense is to connect the dots, and assemble deservedly various pieces of innovation to deliver a complete puzzle: a **studio for multiple innovation**. This organization harnesses projects from business units, intrapreneurs, and cross-BUs projects; it looks up for the next business model, and cooperates with startups. Innately it facilitates **cross-companies innovation**.

Innovation never ceases to reinvent itself, and its role enlarges from new business creation, to agent of change: **transforming the way we work through innovation, what a challenge!** Long life to intrapreneurship, and to Intra-Ventures!

Readings

INTRAPRENEURSHIP

Corporate Entrepreneurship, written by Véronique Bouchard with Alain Fayolle - 2017

Scaling-up Corporate Startups, written by Frank Mattes and Dr. Ralph-Christian Ohr - 2018

Blogs:

- RapidInnovation.fr: blog by Nicolas Bry on Innovation and Intrapreneurship
- Startups2corporate.blogspot.com: blog by Dominique van Deth on Intrapreneurship, Innovation and how it impacts the future of work
- Bimpact assessment.net

White papers, essay & surveys:

- Influence du management de programme intrapreneurial sur le design et l'efficacité des démarches intrapreneuriales, Amélie Moutiers, Université Paris II Panthéon-Assas - 2019
- Intrapreneurship Survey, Dépasser la mythologie des super héros, Institut de l'entreprise et Centre de recherche en gestion (i3-CRG) de l'Ecole polytechnique - 2019
- Grimoire intrapreneuriat - YA+K - 2019

- Intrapreneuriat : recherche collaborative Conseil & Recherche - 2018
- Livre blanc intrapreneuriat, mycrowdcompany - 2018
- 'Transformer votre entreprise de l'intérieur :le guide de l'intrapreneur social by Emmanuel de Lutzel - 2015

INNOVATION MANAGEMENT

- Running Lean: Iterate from plan A to a plan that works - 2012, and Scaling Lean: Mastering the Key Metrics for Startup Growth - 2016, by Ash Maurya
- The Lean Startup: How Constant Innovation Creates Radically Successful Businesses by Eric Ries - 2011
- Business Model Generation: A Handbook for Visionaries, Game Changers, and Challengers by Alexander Osterwalder and Yves Pigneur - 2010

Credits

svgsilh.com : inspiring free icons in creative commons.

P 22 Intrapm Skills Curricu HES
Enterpr

Value Prop + Topol / Orang

BMG

MVP's

Long Perm

MVP   Tilke

BM

Coach's

Disrupt

Made in the USA
Middletown, DE
29 January 2020